SAYING "YES" WISELY

INSIGHTS FOR THE THOUGHTFUL PHILANTHROPIST

With appreciation

29 Ay 2013

Saying "Yes" Wisely:
Insights for the Thoughtful Philanthropist

Copyright © 2009, 2011 Richard Marker

Published by:
Blooming Twig Books
New York / Tulsa
www.bloomingtwig.com

ISBN 978-1-61343-002-6

Former ISBN: 978-1-933918-47-1

Second Edition

Acknowledgments

Most of the essays in this book have been published elsewhere over the last 10 years. All were published under my own copyright or a shared copyright.

For two years, *Stratus Rewards*, a short-lived rewards program for ultra high net worth individuals and families, produced a members-only monthly newsletter for which I was the "philanthropy" expert. Many of the shorter essays in this book appeared on that website. Some have been edited for inclusion here.

Many of the essays were written as op-ed pieces for my blog at: *http://www.WisePhilanthropy.blogspot.com*

"Hubris vs. Humility" was first published in a somewhat different version in *Sh'ma*, October 2001.

"The One Sided Table" was first published in a somewhat different version by *Contact*, Winter 2006.

TABLE OF CONTENTS

SAYING "YES" WISELY

INSIGHTS FOR THE THOUGHTFUL PHILANTHROPIST

BLOOMING TWIG BOOKS
New York / Tulsa

Preface

- June 2011 -

As many readers know, I spent the first 14 years of my career working as a university chaplain, eleven of which were spent at Brown. Eleven years at one university is at least three student generations. Over the time I was there, the very bright creative students who comprised that student population would regularly have "insights" for a great idea that would change the world, or maybe only life on campus. Needless to say, almost all of them were "insights" other students had discovered on a regular basis before them.

One of the important – and really hard – things I had to learn, as a professional advisor, was to resist the temptation to say: "Oh, yes, we tried *that* before," or worse: "Well, *that* idea has *never* worked." For me those initial reactions were evident. For the students whose ideas were newly formulated, such reactions on my part would be terrible. *(True confession: I had to learn this the hard way.)* After all, for these students, what may or may not have happened five years ago was completely beside the point. They hadn't seen it, their friends and peers hadn't seen it, and those were someone else's ideas, not theirs. In other words, if *they* didn't see it, it didn't happen.

In fact, I learned to think: *Who cares if it had been tried before and failed?* What difference would it make if the idea had not accomplished what those other students wanted to accomplish? These students hadn't tried it before and therefore *they* hadn't failed. *They* hadn't gone through the process of learning from their great ideas and insights, in ways that make them wiser and more effective. Isn't that what education is all about?

The real measure of working with or teaching students is that they *learn*. In order to make sure this happens, we professionals must learn to know when to intervene, and when to empower. Empowerment is usually the better option.

I thought of this early career learning in following a bit of a testy exchange on Twitter recently. A very respected and much-better-known colleague in my field responded to an op-ed and blog piece by an assertive self-promoter who is relatively new in our sphere. Her not-hidden scorn was captured by her observation that she had written much the same things a full seven years previously.

I, too, regularly have a reaction to this fellow. He positions himself as if he is the first one to have certain insights on philanthropy or that his philanthropy advisory approach is the first to do things a certain way. Virtually nothing he writes is new and had not been said by many of us, including me, a long time before. My reactions, as that of my colleague, range from frustration to amusement and back to annoyed.

Why do I get so frustrated? I very much doubt that this fellow is plagiarizing. I have no reason to believe he has read any of the essays in this collection or that he had read our mutual colleague's book. As far as he knows, he is saying something new. And while I might like to hope that they would have read *my* previously written words, if his readers learn something new because his are more visible, who am I to begrudge? All of us are committed to advancing and enhancing the world of philanthropy and the thinking of those who give.

Which, in a way, is the underpinning of this reprinting of these essays. Most of the essays still have something to say, can ignite some self-awareness or inspire thinking among those of us who spend our time deciding how, where, and to whom to give.

I am proud to say that in the two years since its first printing, a number of these essays have been quoted elsewhere, and the Marker Method is being used by more and more families and professional advisors.

As with the previous printings, I welcome your feedback, challenges, and your own insights. They are worth hearing, and who knows, they may in fact be brand new contributions to the field that none of us has said or heard before. If so, I promise to give full attribution in future essays.

Introduction

- *August 2009* -

T his is not the introduction I expected to write. Most of the essays in this book were written at a different time. During the economic surge of the last 20 years, the greatest challenge for the affluent (and their foundations) was to learn how to give away their growing wealth – in ways that give them the greatest satisfaction while doing something worthwhile.

Remember those days? It was a wonderful problem. Should one start a new program or support an existing agency? Should one involve one's children and grand-children, and if so, when? Is it better to establish a foundation that lasts into perpetuity or is spent down in one's own lifetime?

There were not simply challenges for the newly wealthy or for those whose wealth grew exponentially. Web 2.0 technologies have allowed those of very modest means to think like the super-rich and to have the same excitement and decision-making choices that previously had been restricted to the very wealthy.

It has been a time when we struggled with under-standing newer hybrid models of solving societal prob-lems, when innovation was funded by venture capitalists who brought the same culture to their philanthropy that they brought to their capital investments, when intergen-erational issues have become pervasive and defining for both non profits and families, and when we have realized the porosity of national borders in addressing social ills.

But as we were putting the final touches on this vol-ume, the world of philanthropy was bombarded. The deepest recession in generations is challenging our thinking about established strategies and priorities. Assets of foundations have been hit hard as have the bank accounts of individuals and families. Even before the radical free fall, I had written some guidelines on how funders might learn from best practices and from the past to navigate these shoals. Many funders had never been asked to make decisions in times of less.

However *l'affaire Madoff* overwhelmed all of that, and had more impact on foundations and non-profits than a year of recession. Some closed, some lost credibility along with assets. Confidence suffered even more. It mandated attention to the responsibilities incumbent on board members, officers, trustees, funders, and their foundations and organizations. It shifted the attention from responsible and effective giving to responsible governance. And most profoundly, it raised a cloud over the trust in this very sector.

Some of the essays in this book address this phenomenon. It is too soon to know, though, if there will be long-term policy or practice changes, or whether this will simply be a passing tragedy. For many it will surely not pass quickly; we don't know if this will have traumatized our sector as a whole. And this collection of essays was put together at the dawning of a new administration in Washington that has its own vision of the role of private philanthropy.

The majority of the essays, though, are not time-bound. They were written over several years for different audiences and different contexts. They have different voices and even some differing styles. Some address events that were current when they were written, and others have insights that apply regardless of the headlines. But a reader will quickly see that there is a consistent point of view, a set of continuing questions, and a vision of what thoughtful and responsible philanthropy is all about.

This book is quite modest in its goals. It does not pretend to reflect brand new research; it believes that there is already much wisdom and proven practice in the philanthropy field; it wishes to enhance and improve more than demand a change and transformation. Some of the material in the essays challenges current orthodoxies, or in the case of the "Marker Method", challenge current most common practices, but these are modest challenges. The goal is to advance and inspire effective private philanthropy and philanthropists. I suspect that many readers will find that there is a homiletic mode to some of the pieces, hopefully without being preachy.

As I write this, I am approaching my mid-60's. Much of my life has been influenced by or involved with philanthropy, either on the giving side or on the recipient side. A few years ago I became conscious that when I was a child, I had many occasions to observe my grandfather, an old-style feel-good philanthropist, spend the last 36 years of his life giving his money away. That early experience was formative. The last 16 years, the latest portion in my career, have found me as a professional funder or an advisor to those who give money away. Each of these direct experiences has added and advanced my knowledge and appreciation for the real value, potential, and work of philanthropy.

Nothing enables understanding greater than teaching. When I began lecturing nationally and teaching funders at the New York University Academy for Grantmaking and Funder Education, my own knowledge expanded exponentially. And continues to do so. Our "students" are themselves philanthropists or professional funders. One cannot be cavalier about one's knowledge when standing in front of those who continue to be on the front lines. Thanks to Naomi Levine for allowing the development of this division of NYU's George Heyman Jr. Center for Philanthropy and Fundraising and also to my fellow faculty whose own excellence and depth of knowledge of the field make sure that we continue to be offering a state of the art educational opportunity.

The nature of my work and social connections is that I have become intimately familiar with many families and foundations doing, or wishing to do, wonderful things with the resources at their disposal. These relationships may be brief, but they are always robust and instructive; they are often moving as well. Truth be told, my proximity to so many philanthropists and foundations has also exposed me to many who don't do it well or whose egos or arrogance get in the way. In many cases, I have built both the good and bad situations into the cases or examples I use widely – I am careful to disguise these so that none of those referred to have ever identified themselves. I mention none of my clients by name – for reasons that I am sure need not be articulated here.

There are, though, a very small number of people who have been integral to getting this book to this stage. Donald Jonas is a very admirable philanthropist whom I know socially and casually. It was he who, in a conversation, expressed surprise that I hadn't yet committed my extensive range of thinking to a book. Little did he know that his passing comment came at just the right moment. It demonstrates how life's fleeting moments can have a lasting effect.

We have had a long-lasting relationship with Edith Everett, and with her late husband, Henry. My wife Mirele considers Edith her mentor, going back to a time early in her career when the Everett Foundation funded the project that gave Mirele her professional distinctiveness and reputation. Since then, they, and now she, have become cherished friends, and models of thoughtful, courageous, caring and insightful philanthropy. Many of much greater means would do well to learn from them about when and how to do grant-making that pushes the envelope, leverages resources, and carefully maneuvers between long and short-term kinds of funding. Edith and Henry never were or will Edith ever be a client, but I learn constantly about the very best of philanthropy from our continuing conversations.

Anyone who knows us as a couple knows that Mirele is my beloved life and business partner. Anyone who knows Mirele as a person knows that she is philanthropy incarnate. Her love of human-kind, her belief that the world can and must be better, and her enthusiastic and energetic commitment to giving more of herself than we can ever give from our financial means are the daily influences which give meaning to my own life and work.

The book is now yours, but the work is far from finished. So I invite readers to share their stories and to challenge the insights contained herein. Only by continuing to learn from so many will I be able to continue to help others "say 'yes' wisely." In advance, thanks.

Section I:
Philanthropy in Our Time: Trends & Theory

T here is no political, religious, or social system anywhere that doesn't see a role for some sort of philanthropy. It can be the collection plate, the charity box, mandatory "volunteering", large scale institution building, or taking care of whole families of household workers. The understandings can be personal altruism, a commitment to fixing the world, a replacement for government inadequacy or a belief in the inappropriateness of government funding.

For many reasons, philanthropy has moved to center stage today. Globalism, for all of its challenges, has made us aware of the interrelatedness of the world's needs – and given rise to philanthropy not limited by borders. The destruction of the earth's eco-structure is not restrained by national borders, calling for assertive advocacy to save us all. Systemic inequities call for systemic solutions; many thoughtful givers are attempting to fund underlying issues and not simply provide surface palliatives. The limitation of public funding has forced the question of the role of philanthropy to supplement government funding – throughout the world. And the opportunity for philanthropic innovation has led to new solutions to educational, artistic, scientific, and medical challenges.

New high visibility philanthropists such as Warren Buffet, Bill and Melinda Gates, and Michael Bloomberg have pushed philanthropic giving onto the front pages.

And the use of cyberspace to stimulate giving for those with smaller checking accounts – in an empowering and engaging way – has begun to change the landscape.

When many of these essays were written, philanthropy had become a well-meaning plaything of the newly wealthy; new modes of giving, expectations for outcomes, experimentations with for-profit and non-profit hybrid models had overwhelmed the umbrella charities which had dominated the charitable landscape for the last two generations. When the more recent group of essays was written, so much of that wealth had eroded that questions of giving in times of less became a dominant theme and concern. Thoughtful givers will ask the same question regardless of the underlying economic conditions: what is the role of philanthropy, and what does it say about our human nature and our national character.

Chapter 1:
The Role of Philanthropy in Our World

Accountability & Necessity
(American philanthropy in the 21st century)

Over the past year, there has been much noise, and some rare clarity of voice, in public discourse regarding the role of philanthropy in the public weal.

It hasn't been the best of times for the philanthropic community. It has proven itself every bit as susceptible to guile, avarice, and self-importance as the business community.[1] I don't know how extensive abuse of public trust will prove to have been in the business community; I suspect that, in the philanthropic community, it will be shown that the good far exceeds the rotten.

And, to make matters worse, these affronts and abuses have come at a time of tremendous challenges to philanthropic resources. Despite the profound gains in last year's stock market, it is a rare foundation or major funder with the dispensable income of 2 or 3 years ago. History tells us that, even with a rebound in the economy, the philanthropic enterprise will trail the economy by 2 or 3 years.

The challenge is compounded yet further by the government's recent attention to philanthropy. Not surprising if one thinks about it. After all, our national debt has exploded at the cost of human services. Where might one find relief? One has the sense that politicians are viewing foundations with a Willie Sutton perspective -

---

[1] Perhaps not so surprising since most philanthropic foundations have as their base, resources from individuals who have made those fortunes in the business world, and are typically governed by those same people and their families and close advisors.

that's where the money is. If one has exempted the wealthiest individuals, beneficiaries of both tremendous tax relief and the most immediate beneficiaries of an economic rebound, philanthropic foundations, donor advised funds, and the like are a repository of substantial and enticing dollars. Why not shift the burden of responsibility for human need to those quasi private and now suspect institutions? Why allow a permanent endowment?

Thus we come to the essential issue. What is the role of the philanthropic sector in this century? Is it to provide for society's safety net or should that continue to be a governmental responsibility? Is it to provide a permanent risk capital fund to respond to unimagined future needs or to be used to immediate identified needs? Is it to provide the venture capital for innovative and untested responses to medical, cultural, educational, and social challenges or is it to provide for operating support for existing and established responses? Should the flexibility for making these choices be in the hands of donors, who, because of skill, genetics, or good fortune, have amassed the means to establish philanthropic vehicles, or should the parameters of the role of philanthropy be circumscribed by political considerations – often unrelated to charitable motivations?

My experience on both sides of the philanthropic divide at different times, as an executive on the donor side and also the not-for-profit agency side, I am convinced that we need the visionary aspects of philanthropy more than ever. Philanthropists and foundations need to have the flexibility to choose permanence or the immediate; they need to be able to think out of the box and risk failure in order to challenge and change existing orthodoxies – or to sustain wonderful and worthy well established institutions. They need to be free to bring the most creative thinking of entrepreneurs and the most sophisticated thinking of professionals to bear on the wide range of social issues – free of the constraints of political considerations. America needs to allow the unique and distinct role of philanthropy to flourish precisely at a time when the pressure is to reign in their independence. To be sure, philanthropists and foundations must be accountable to the highest ethical and moral standards; that should not be confused with holding them to undue restrictions on endowments and spending policies that limit their ability to impact society.

As a philanthropic advisor and educator about philanthropy, I have had numerous occasions to speak to groups of government and NGO leaders from other countries. They admire and envy the extraordinary role of philanthropy so well developed in the United States. They wonder how to learn from the voluntary sector to make changes in their own countries. To be sure, there are lessons about universal health care and pensions that we might learn from other industrialized countries, and we should celebrate and sustain the unique institutions that characterize the voluntary sector in the United States. For all of the noise, and oft-times legitimate challenges to this sector of the past months, philanthropy must continue to play its visionary and visible role in the century so painfully now underway.

Chapter 1-A:
Setting the Tone

S eems pretty direct... Those who need, ask. Those who have, give. What's so complicated, or more to the point, what is so hard about that? In the introduction to the first section, we spoke of the profound change to the nature of American philanthropy that followed the New Deal. Intended or not, it precipitated the philanthropic landscape we know today. One needn't be a Rockefeller or a Bloomberg to be solicited regularly in every medium possible – snail mail, email, and telephone.

This next set of essays can be read as setting the tone and attitude for those of us, all of us, who give money away. As we see from the very first essay, originally written as an online holiday-season piece, giving is not primarily about how much one gives but how we do it and how we feel about it.

The second essay in this section, which was originally published in a slightly different version by *Sh'ma* has been quoted more than any other I have written over the years. Funders can sometimes forget what their giving means and how they are perceived. In my teaching, I emphasize how to learn to distinguish between the influence of the funder and the abuse of the power of the funder. It is a delicate balance, for which humility is an indispensable part.

The next two essays, originally published in the *Stratus Rewards* online magazine, tell us that philanthropic giving need be motivated by what can be accomplished and not simply by a negotiated dollar amount. Since business people typically want to "buy low, sell high" it is tempting to act the same way in our philanthropic giving. These essays remind us that there are very different bottom lines.

How often do we hear the expression "sitting at the table" to represent enfranchisement and empowerment? The next essay attempts, in metaphoric fashion, to acknowledge that all of these tables aren't the same, the interests of the funders aren't always the same, and the relationship with grantees is constantly evolving. With so many new forms of giving, it may be useful to pause to see which side we are actually sitting on.

Finally, all of us on the giving side know what it has felt like to be a walking dollar sign. How well we balance that strangely shaped crown tells a lot about us, and goes a long way to demonstrating how we intend to have others treat us. We cannot control their instincts, but we can control our own.

Giving & Gifting

- December 5th, 2004 -

'Tis the season.... For gifting and giving.

Gifting focuses on the object; giving is about the subject.

Gifting answers the question how much we give; giving shows how much we care.

Gifting satisfies our lists; giving satisfies our life.

Gifting fulfils our responsibility; giving expands our sensibilities;

Charitable gifting rewards our bottom line; philanthropic giving celebrates our highest values.

Gifting changes the mood; giving changes the world.

Gifting expresses our generosity; giving expresses our love.

May the holiday season teach us that the best gift of all is truly giving of oneself. It is the gift that gives back, and brings joy to both the giver and the recipient.

May the New Year be one of blessings, good health, and prosperity... and may the world become a better place by our example and our generosity of spirit.

Hubris or Humility

- June 2001 -

It was during my job interview with Edgar M. Bronfman when I learned philanthropy's first lesson. "We need someone who will know how to say no to all of these wonderful causes in a gracious manner," he told me. There are so many worthy and deserving causes, caring and thoughtful people, genuine unmet needs and powerful but untested ideas. Many more than any philanthropist or foundation can possibly fund. It is indeed important to say "no" graciously. It was gratifying when, in my third week on the job, I received a call from someone who told me that he had never received a rejection that made him feel so good.

Faced with so many requests, I appreciate that our foundation has priorities and policies to determine which projects are eligible for consideration. In the case of most requests, it is intellectually easy to say no, since they simply don't fit. Emotionally, it is much harder. Individuals' destinies and dreams are in your hands. Institutions' missions are on the line. Social welfare and the social weal can be influenced by a nod or a no. Cutting edge thinking can be legitimated by an endorsement, or relegated to triviality by a rejection. There is a power in the role of the funder, which I experience on a daily basis, and which reinforces the following lessons:

Lesson #1: Our answer has an impact on the lives of so many. The more one must say no, the more humility one must have.

As difficult as it is to say "no" graciously, it is even harder to say "yes" wisely. In reviewing eligible proposals, the decisions become even harder. In my career, I have been an executive in the not-for-profit sector, taught at the university level, consulted in the for-profit sector, and served on a wide variety of boards. Yet, as a foundation executive, I am continually struck by how little I know. There are seemingly wonderful projects which we cannot adequately evaluate because we lack the expertise, and whose worth cannot be proven unless a funder takes a chance. Some ideas and projects might change the world, or at least some small part of it; others will be failures, glorious or otherwise. Some are prestigious and safe; others might become the next great thing. With limited funds and more limited prophecy at our disposal, each approved grant is a well-placed bet. With all of the analytic abilities that trustees, program officers, and evaluators bring to bear, it is always human judgment that is the final arbiter. Thus...

Lesson #2: Every grant reminds me that nothing is guaranteed. With humility, we rely on our best judgment to decide and on others to implement what only the future will demonstrate to be true.

If I am aware of my limited expertise, others are always telling me how wise, insightful, thoughtful, helpful, unique I am. When I first moved to this side of the table, I was convinced that they must be correct. It felt wonderful that all of my fine attributes were finally being recognized. Fortunately for our foundation, flattery didn't guarantee a grant. And I quickly learned that my much-heralded attributes were less appreciated when a grant was not forthcoming. Ah, humbling.

Lesson #3: Don't confuse who you are with what (or whom)   you represent.

The last lesson is the most important and transcendent of all. It is an extraordinary blessing to be in a position to make a difference. It is all too easy, with so many wanting so much, to take our good fortune for granted, to become insensitive to real need, or worst of all, to become haughty with the power in our hands. That would be both sad and wrong. It is important never to forget, as the one on whom luck, skill, or destiny bestowed the bounty of this world, or as their professional representative, that it is a rare privilege to engage in philanthropy. Its very meaning, the love of humankind, must inform all of our actions and affect.

Lesson #4: Our vision, therefore, must be dictated by the mandate to make the world a better place through the resources we dispense.

History will judge us by how well we respond to this unique challenge and gift. And that is the most humbling lesson of all.

Fund for Success

- May 17ᵗʰ, 2004 -

I t was 1973. The paper of record had a photograph of a titan in business and philanthropy handing over a $1 million check to a worthy charity. The scion of this family was an undergraduate at Brown, where I was working at the time. Everyone congratulated this young heir – whose response was, "My father always says, 'No one gives 'til it hurts.'"

For many years, I saw that story as an example of the greater potential of wealthy Americans to use their affluence for good. Lately though, as I advise more and more families and foundations, I have concluded that there is a corollary: "Very few give 'til it helps."

In business, one always tries to maximize income while reducing expenses. Shouldn't the same be true for one's philanthropic investments? Why give more than necessary? Shouldn't one negotiate a gift down to a more reasonable level? Surely the beseeching organization has inflated its need and costs to encourage greater generosity – and just as surely they expect you to bargain.

But, isn't that the wrong question? When we invest in a business venture, we examine the financials to make sure that there is a likelihood of a healthy return. Adequate capitalization is one of the measures. We typically don't ask how little they need, but how much capital is necessary to succeed.

The same is true in the not-for-profit world. A shrewd donor may persuade an organization that they can get by with less of his or her philanthropic dollars. But if the organization cannot accomplish all of its potential because of undercapitalization, we have not invested well. Due diligence should investigate potential as well as legitimacy.

Philanthropists need to fund for success, not simply efficiency.

Fund for Success ≠ Fund Success

- July 23rd, 2009 -

The previous article articulates what many readers and those who have heard me speak and teach about grantmaking know, one of my mantras is that funders should "fund for success."

My intention in this formulation is to challenge the tendency of many funders to ask how little they need to give for a project. They often assume that a grant request is padded and the grantseeker has built in an expectation of a discounted grant amount.

Funders are not unreasonable in thinking this way. It is certainly true that there is a long history of grantseekers assuming that they will never get all that they ask for so they pad. It is also true that funders want their money to go further so they choose to give less, but to more recipients. Reasonable.

What is also true is a more challenging cultural reality. Let's be honest. Most funders made their money the old fashioned way: they "bought low and sold high." They negotiated the best deals, putting the least possible investment with the greatest possible return. Not a bad way to make money. Not surprising at all that funders then apply the same thinking to their grantmaking – as if it is a negotiation. Thus the mentality that funders respond to funding requests with the reply with the functional equivalent question of "how little can I give you and still do the project?"

However, grantmaking is not the same thing as a business negotiation. Or more to the point, it should be more in line with the full due diligence which a businessperson is likely to do. The questions that funders should ask when looking at a grant request is not "how little" is needed to pull off a project but rather what is necessary for a project to succeed. A funder should have as much at stake as a recipient that a proposed funded project succeed and is properly capitalized. To be sure, sometimes that may mean that a request is overblown, that a careful analysis shows that the requisite amount for a project to succeed is indeed less than what was stated in the request.

However, there are many times when a request understates its needs – that, reluctant to ask for what would really make a difference or perhaps naïve about their own real needs, the grantseeker is actually understating what would be required to have a project or program achieve its potential. It is here that the mantra "fund for success" really applies. A funder with commitment to a project can truly reshape a request so that the grantee can fulfill its aspirations and the funder can see the results of the investment. There may even be times when it is appropriate and prudent to give more than that requested when this principle is applied.

This concept is not so new or radical, and has been applied by many knowledgeable funders for a long time. But it does catch some by surprise and newer funders often need to learn to focus their thinking on grantee relations to become good partners.

Last week, though, I learned that my mantra can be – and perhaps has been - misunderstood: one very experienced and knowledgeable foundation exec assumed that my message of "fund for success" was that funders should only fund projects with a high likelihood of success, that they should eschew risk wherever possible. He rebutted that funders should be very open to risk in certain circumstances and have a high failure tolerance.

As it happens, I fully agree with him and am taking this opportunity to address any misunderstanding. I profoundly wish that funders were less risk averse and that they were more open to failure. I don't believe that only

funding safe "successful" projects is an ideal or necessarily a preferred way to fund. Private philanthropy is
the risk capital of a society, and as such there needs to be
a healthy dose of thoughtful risk taking in the work we
do.

Funding FOR success is not the same as only funding
successful and safe projects. It means that we should
fund whatever we fund with an eye toward what a project truly needs and not simply what a proposal asks for.
If it fails, with all of the best thought and planning, so be
it; let's learn from that failure to fund another day. But to
only fund safely is too often [not always] the preserva-
tion of mediocrity or that which is less interesting.

Chapter 1-B:
America and the World

Normal Philanthropy
(distinguishes American philanthropy)

One of my colleagues on the faculty at NYU's Center for Philanthropy is Claire Gaudiani, the author of *The Greater Good: How Philanthropy Drives the American Economy and Can Save Capitalism*. Her challenging and somewhat controversial book argues that the not-for-profit sector has been an indispensable component of the uniqueness of the American experience and a key driver of American economic success.

While our approaches are somewhat different, she and I agree on one significant understanding of philanthropy in America. The real story of American philanthropy is not the "bold face" names; Astor, Carnegie, Rockefeller, or Rosenwald, or even Annenberg or Gates. These Croesus level philanthropists have done extraordinary things with their wealth, but there have been aristocratic or royal funders elsewhere in the world who have established foundations in Europe, Asia, and Latin America. This doesn't diminish their philanthropy, just their uniqueness.

What distinguishes American philanthropy is that most Americans feel a responsibility to give; to churches or synagogues, to neighborhood centers, to cancer funds, to tsunami relief, to symphonies, to the homeless and hungry, to universities and museums, or special projects of our own choosing.

I like to call this "normal philanthropy," the philanthropy that all of us, no matter what our means, can and should participate in. No one has enough money to do everything, and everyone has enough to do something.

It is what distinguishes the American charitable impulse from many other countries. It is a legacy that honors us all.

The Power of Small Gifts
(uniqueness of American philanthropy)

- March 16ᵗʰ, 2008 -

Readers of my articles, and those who have heard me speak, know that I believe that the uniqueness of American philanthropy is *not* that our society is more generous than others, nor that the story of philanthropy is best told by viewing the giving of the super-rich. Such philanthropy has been a part of every society and, while interesting and even vicariously stimulating, is hardly the model for "the rest of us."

It is my pleasure to refer you to a newsletter published by a very fine firm that does similar work to my own. The subject of the March 2008 issue of the newsletter of *The Philanthropic Initiative (TPI)* focuses on the power of small gifts. I am pleased to refer that newsletter to you as a fine collection of successful models for the overwhelming majority of us who have limited funds that we would like to use for good. See *www.tpi.org*.[2]

In my own experience, I have been inspired by those who have given impactfully and effectively with very limited means; for example, the undergraduates who, while volunteering in a public school, learned that the budget for arts had been excised.

They learned that for merely $250 per month they could provide supplies to keep the arts programming going. That is, for a mere $5 per week, undergraduates

---

[2] On a more personal level, I want to acknowledge Ellen Remmer, *TPI*'s CEO, who encouraged me to go public with my thinking and publish more after hearing me speak at a conference in 2002. Several steps removed, she deserves credit for this volume. She is a wonderful colleague.

were able to sustain what the school system couldn't. They committed themselves to give or raise that amount. For less than the cost of a movie, about the same as a fancy multi-fashioned cup of coffee, or a single foot-long sub sandwich these creative and caring young people demonstrated how to be a philanthropist on $5 per week!

Or what about the person who took our NYU classes with but one purpose: to learn how to establish her limited purpose foundation. The purpose: to provide a single college scholarship for a graduate of her high school. This person was not wealthy, a mid-level executive with no dependents or direct heirs. Her own lifetime needs already accounted for, she wanted to do one thing which could make a difference within her means. She is a philanthropist by any definition.

One cannot be a member of the board of the NY Philharmonic for $500; but for $500 one can provide enough to put a start-up on the map. Last year, a group of 20-somethings chose to produce a concert to support a young environmental organization. They asked us to "sponsor" the reception after the concert. It was a wonderful concert and one of the most gratifying $500 gifts we ever made.

Youth philanthropy is, almost by definition, "small gifts." Youth philanthropy collaboratives rarely give more than $1000 to any one cause or organization. $1000 doesn't get much attention from the CEO of a major non-profit organization, yet I have yet to meet a non profit CEO who would not meet with a group of teens doing due diligence. Those who choose to provide challenge or matching gifts to youth philanthropy programs are among the proudest funders I have ever met.

Small gifts => Big impact => Bigger gratification.

American Exceptionalism?

- June 15ᵗʰ, 2008 -

L ater this week, I will be in Jerusalem speaking to 100 leading philanthropists from Australia, South Africa, Europe, Latin America, and Canada. Not by coincidence, none will be from the United States. The sponsoring organization works throughout much of the world excluding the United States, so the make-up of the group is as one would have expected.

My assigned topic, intergenerational philanthropy, is one that fits easily into my realm of expertise, and it was flattering indeed to be asked to make this presentation. And, even though I most assuredly live and do most of my work in the United States, I have spoken on five continents and have had many years of professional experience working with those in other nations. Yet one of the assignments from the organizers continues to lurk. Please, they said, don't discuss the United States.

It is an intriguing challenge, but one which reflects interesting perceptions about American exceptionalism. Implicit are a whole range of assumptions: about American imperialist tendencies even in philanthropy, about the American self misperception that we are uniquely philanthropic and charitable, about the ambivalence much of the rest of the world has in coming to grips with profound challenges to societal assumptions by younger generations,[3] of the complex nature of the NGO sectors in many countries as contrasted with the non profit sector in the USA, differing government, social, and eco-

---

[3] Of which there may be as many as 3 or even 4 depending on how one counts.

nomic histories and their role in providing for social service or quality of life support.

This is not a new set of questions and I want to acknowledge the important contributions of so many of my colleagues to more in-depth and informed understanding of the topic. Not surprisingly, there isn't universal agreement on the findings and, more importantly, there is tremendous variation both within regions and across regions. I for one have always advocated that we learn best from one another by following the dictum "Adapt, don't adopt." Nevertheless, from my experience, there does seem to be one area that transcends borders and boundaries:

While it is true that social systems, the role of government, and the tax systems may indeed influence the *structures* of how one gives, the *decision-making process* within families, corporations, and foundations is remarkably analogous. Factors such as anonymity vs. recognition, local vs. broader concerns, who should be involved in making decisions, how involved one might choose to be in a cause, selecting grantees best aligned with one's values, and numerous others, become central once one has decided to give.

There is no doubt that there are profound differences between generations, and marked differences across cultures, but when it comes down to one's altruistic impulse, our questions, if not our answers, reflect one common humanity.

My meetings this week, which will be non-American and not even reflect a single cultural tradition, will help me determine what more there is to learn from one another, and what else we share. Stay tuned...

What Did I Learn from the International Philanthropists?

- June 29, 2008 -

T hey were from Latin America, Canada, Europe, Israel, South Africa, and Australia. All of them were committed to philanthropy, and all of them eager to learn. My job was to translate the transformative elements of 21st Century philanthropy (and identity) to folks who successfully mastered the 20th. I was to address the challenges of the generations.

What was so refreshing, for me, was their openness. There was much less dismissiveness and defensiveness than one might have imagined. After all, these were people who had earned the right to be leaders; in their own communities, in their nations and international organizations. They had put their time, energy, and money on the table for many years. And they were being challenged by, of all things, an American. It would hardly have surprised me had they responded otherwise. They wouldn't have been the first group of senior funders who have wished that the world would be as it used to be, and that the organizations they built would be embraced by their offspring.

There were a couple of areas about which there was some disagreement. One example was about the significance of tax policies to private giving. There were clear cultural differences between different parts of the world.

But more than disagreement was genuine concern and puzzlement. For them, as for most senior communal leaders, commitment means loyalty and affiliation as the manifestations of identity. "What does it mean to believe in a cause," they asked, "if younger people don't feel that they need to 'belong' or have long-term financial commitment or even the sense of responsibility to work for an organization? Isn't organizational involvement the very manifestation of caring for a cause or community? Otherwise, isn't it simply an indulgence?"

Of course, those of us in this world accept that this is precisely the intergenerational divide. For newer funders, loyalty persuades less than performance, and proven results trump marketing messages. Why support an organization just because it has been around for a while and once may have been great? And why support (reputed) bloated bureaucracies when direct-targeted grants will go directly to those in need?

I found most moving that the group of senior philanthropists I was meeting with had already accepted that the world was moving beyond them. As one of the most respected leaders emphasized in his concluding comments on my words, "In my family, we have been having these discussions for a long time. Our philanthropy has changed because of it. The younger members simply don't want to do it my way any longer." These leaders really do care about being relevant and not just being honored. They really do want to find ways to convey their deepest values and caring to those who follow.

For the last several years, in my teaching and talking, I have spoken about a time of transition, between that which was, to that which will be. This session with these 100 international philanthropists persuaded me that that isn't the question any longer. It is the new era that already fully defines us.

Korean Philanthropy
(compared to American philanthropy)

- December 20, 2007 -

I t is always flattering to be interviewed for a TV network, but this was the first time it was for a Korean audience. The questions were certainly as telling as my answers were interesting (of course). Their assumptions about American philanthropy and generosity assumed the truth of American exceptionalism: that Americans as a people are more generous than other nations. The example they gave was the widely publicized "coat drive" appeal being heard on all radio and TV stations in the New York area.[4]

At the end of the interview, it was clear that their motivation was to encourage Koreans to learn to be more philanthropic and to strengthen the voluntary sector in South Korea. They pointed out that, in Korea, 80% of philanthropic giving comes from corporations and only 20% from individuals, whereas the inverse seems to apply here.

There is indeed much to learn from American philanthropy, but not all of it is necessarily complimentary. While it is true that most Americans feel some commitment to give voluntarily, it is also true that, in the USA, there is no assumption that the public/government sector is the first place to turn for human need. In most other industrialized/modern societies, the assumption is that

---

[4] It is true that Americans have a highly developed institutional third sector; it is less clear, as readers of this blog know, that Americans are in fact more generous than others around the world.

human need is first and foremost a public responsibility. But in the USA, many feel that, if not for their personal support, the homeless will be on the streets and the hungry will not be fed. People can differ on which reflects the more caring vision for society.

At the same time, even societies which feel that the public sector should provide for human needs recognize the limits of the ability of any government to provide for all needs in an open ended way. No nation is rich enough for that. There certainly is still the role for private philanthropy to add to those services or to be the place for innovation and change. It is indeed a good thing for all individuals to feel the commitment to voluntarism, both financially and otherwise. If Korean society could adapt the best of our philanthropy to its own reality, it would surely be a stronger society.

One last point: the interviewer asked me what role the private/corporate sector might play in advancing this vision. I replied that it is not enough for corporations to serve their own image by strategically placed contributions. Really good corporate citizenship encourages employee giving, through matching funds, time released volunteerism, and loaned executives for the NGO sector. Attitudes and behaviors can change – if there are communal values that inform them.

Chapter Two:

Philanthropy in a Time of Change

N o reader of these essays need be reminded that the world is changing around us. Some of these changes reflect political and economic changes; others are of a longer lasting and ultimately more profound nature. The short-term changes of the economic collapse challenge funding practices; the long-term, not yet fully defined changes will impact public policy; the most transformative of these changes re-define the very way in which we live, communicate, and understand civil society.

These next several essays address some of these issues. As with all of the essays in this book, they were written at different times, in response to different moments, and have different emphases. All speak to a time of profound change. More than any of the other essays in this book, they will need to be revised, rethought, and expanded over time. Surely the responses of you readers will help shape those revisions for future editions. I welcome your thoughts.

Old Wine in New Bottles

- September 18th, 2008 -

One of the great fun perks of working as an executive of Seagram, when it still existed, was a very extensive "product allowance." Since the company was one of the largest importers of premium and estate wines, simply put, this meant that I could buy lots of fine wine at company expense. I regret that very little of the very ample supply from those years remains, but it was a great run. I do have one bottle that I keep as a keepsake. When the company cellar was being closed, we had the opportunity to select some for ourselves. Among my selections were 2 bottles of a 1964 *Haut-Brion*. Oenophiles will recognize the label. A few years ago, on a special occasion, we drank one of them. Its extraordinary quality was evident, but it was clear that it was reaching the end of its cellar shelf life. The other will sit unopened as a token (although I guess I would entertain an interesting offer from a real collector).

I was reminded about this wine during two recent visits and speaking engagements. Not infrequently, organizations invite me to comment on changes in the philanthropic environment – presumably as a way to get into the mind of funders as they consider the profound societal and economic changes which impact all of us. Makes a lot of sense... Since I know very little about fundraising, my commentary is never about how these organizations can get more money, but they find my approach useful, if challenging, to hear the perspective of the other side.

It is also fairly typical that some of the leaders of these organizations – committed and passionate about what they do, have done, and would like to continue to do – suggest that in fact the real problem is "marketing." Their challenge, they say, is to re-brand, to market to a new generation of potential funders, or re-package what they do. If they do so, they believe the funds would flow.

These responses are well meaning but miss the point. It assumes that the 21st century is simply the last century re-packaged. But it isn't. We are living through one of the transformational moments in history. A snail mail letter is quaint, but it isn't email. A newspaper is solid, comprehensive, and sometimes even noble. But it isn't a web-search or a blog. You may argue that one is better than the other, but that isn't the point; the point is that the new technology is different and now predominant. Even if one can make the case that the quality of a hard copy letter is higher, more thoughtful, and often has the benefit of being more considered, we aren't going to see a return to that being the way in which most personal or business communication takes place.

This isn't the place to restate the full range of the changes in polity, epistemology, authority, relationship, community that we are living through. (After all, that is what people pay me to talk about.) But when I hear organizational leaders articulate to me that the way in which they will inspire future generations of funders and leaders is to re-brand, I am quite sure that they are already relegating themselves to yesterday's news. Sometimes I do hear from visionary or thoughtful leaders who acknowledge that they understand the dilemma facing them and wonder how to maneuver into the future without discarding a well earned past reputation. While they may not be able to stem the onslaught of change, they are more likely to be open to rethinking and reinventing than their peers who cannot quite see it.

In the non-profit world, the truest responses are the new enterprises, the social entrepreneurs, the independent risk takers, all of whom emerge organically from understanding and experiencing a different world. The best of them don't try to look for places at the table or to

define themselves within the vocabulary of the successful organizations of the 20th Century. They all identify
real interests, needs, solutions, and communities that
simply look different than the past. Some, perhaps even
most of these social entrepreneurs will fail; and to be
sure not every innovation is transformative. But we already know that there are those who imagine a world
different than the one they were born into, and who create ways of doing and being that are nothing less than
transformative.

The *Haut-Brion* bottle is, for me, a wonderful keepsake of a time gone by. But it has gone by. The quality
of its wine in its time cannot be overstated. But it is yesterday's wine. Pouring that wine into new bottles would
neither honor the quality of the vintage, nor would it entice a new generation of wine drinkers to purchase the
old and now likely out of date contents.

Will the Obama Moment Move Philanthropy?

- January 22ⁿᵈ, 2009 -

Leading up to this week's inauguration, lots of us in the philanthropy field have been interviewed or asked to speak about the new Obama administration. Most of those conversations have focused on policy and legislation. Much has been written, including a very impressive compilation of ideas in the Chronicle of Philanthropy some weeks ago. I congratulate my colleagues on the scope of their thinking. I too have been interviewed and quoted on my expectations and desires regarding these changes.

Needless to say, most of the comments have been expressed under an extra thick cloud. The precipitous deterioration in the economy and the resultant fragility of the social weal mean that there are fewer dollars available for greater need. And the embarrassment of recent scandals have jeopardized the confidence that resources given for public good are safe, secure, and responsibly managed for the purpose for which they exist.

Inevitably laws that will create incentives for private giving, increased accountability and transparency to the 3rd sector, and recalibration of the relative roles of private philanthropy and public policy will be on the congressional table. There is a very long list of proposals floating around which address all of these.[5]

This posting is being written in the glow of this extraordinary week when the world sat still, filled with

---

[5] For those of you who are interested in my opinion about any of these proposals, please feel free to be in touch.

positive aspiration, awed admiration, and jubilant anticipation. The Obama moment is not simply a time for policy reconsideration, though it is indeed that. It is at least as much a time for attitudinal adjustment; for a reconsideration of our own involvements, commitments, and expectations.

The question I have been struggling with is, "Will this aura change the way people do their philanthropy?" It is quite early but here are a few thoughts:

1. *Transparency and accountability*

The ethics mandates for the executive branch should remind funders that there really is a difference between abuse of power and the legitimate exercise of influence. The insistence on accountability should remind funders that conflict of interest laws, prudent investor rules, etc., are worth taking seriously, not only because it is the law but because it is right.

2. *Collaboration*

In recent weeks, at least two dozen foundations have asked for my guidelines for collaborations and partnerships among funders. Is it possible that the theme of common challenges will translate into a new commitment by funders to work together? Some of this is surely motivated by leveraging fewer dollars; some, I suspect is also because it is a new day.

3. *Commitment to success*

As surprising as this may sound, many funders continue to view the relationship with grantees as a negotiating process. Many others, particularly younger funders, view the funder-grantee relationship as one that must make a difference. Therefore they ask different questions, require different information, and fund in different ways. They want their money to help grantees succeed, not simply exist. It is time for the relationships between funders and grantees to be defined by that joint commitment, recognizing that it emphasizes the symbiosis between the two sides.

4. *Service*

For the past generation, the US economy has moved into one of providing service, not manufacturing product. I suspect that there will be a new definition of the service industry, one that makes voluntarism a norm and not an exception. I particularly anticipate that there will be new national service programs for the late career "actives", that pre-college gap programs will become highly recommended, that funders will be likely to paint and pay, especially during these next couple of years of difficult economic times. There will be wonderful opportunities for funders to enable this to happen.

5. *Connection between domestic & worldwide need*

No serious economist pretends that we can or should live in a purely national economic system. Philanthropy should function in much the same way. Fortunately, a number of our most visible and prestigious philanthropists have already demonstrated their understanding of this. I would hope that we can simplify our philanthropy systems around the world to make fighting hunger, poverty, suffering, and environmental destruction more seamless across borders.

6. *Optimism*

Because philanthropy is voluntary, it is the reflection of society's deepest values. Perhaps most important of all will be the sense that our time, our money, our work and our passions can make a difference. The philanthropic sector can capture the tone of this time to create a melody of moment, one that not only addresses needs but enables dreams. It is certainly possible that a visionary philanthropy sector will become a leading force for change, when so many are committed to try. And maybe, in fact, that is exactly what we are about.

The Roubini Effect

- June 4, 2009 -

Earlier this week, I had the intellectual pleasure [but the emotional let down] of hearing a far-reaching economic assessment by Nouriel Roubini. Professor Roubini is well known for his dour assessment and he didn't surprise the assemblage of well-healed and largely high net-worth attendees. While Prof. Roubini and I both teach at NYU, this was the first time we had met. His reputation for breadth of knowledge is well deserved, although his pessimism hardly left anyone very cheery – even on a magnificent spring day high above Manhattan.

I am not a trained economist, so I am hardly equipped to rebut any of Roubini's points. However, as I heard him, it seemed that even he does not predict a repeat of the perfect storm of economic catastrophe that caused the worldwide implosion of the last 18 months. While he emphasizes the negatives, he allows for the possibility that some of the initiatives which have been taken are not fully off base and may even work. As one in the philanthropy field, I am always on the side of the improvable, not the inevitable, so I will grasp at the few positive straws which Roubini waves around.

Which brings me to the main point of this posting. At this luncheon I was seated next to a person whose family last name is known by all. Over lunch, this individual, who has at his disposal some of the most well-known and prestigious philanthropy advice around, peppered me with questions about the trends and probabilities in this world. I honestly don't think that he was looking for new information as much as reflecting, through his questions, the continuing unsettled feeling that all philanthropists feel these days.

For example, it is clear that 2009 will be a much harder year for philanthropic giving than the last. As I have written previously, foundation giving and large individual gifts are almost always prospective pledges based on retrospective assets. If a pledge was based on assets in January 2008, by the time that was paid the asset base was probably quite a bit smaller – but the pledge will still be paid based on assets at the time of the pledge. Similarly, a pledge made in Spring 2009 will probably be based on assets in hand now. So even should there be a remarkable recovery by December, the pledge will be based on current assets, not potential ones. I cannot imagine a scenario in which the non-profit world will see improvements for at least another year, except, perhaps, for those which may qualify for new government funding.

Similarly, by now all major funders have addressed what to do with a smaller asset base. They have made the hard decisions and are implementing them. The range of responses has been addressed in previous posts, but by this time, we have seen virtually any of the possibilities play out – from increasing payout to more focus to continuing the course to non-financial support to new partnerships..... Why then did this boldface name ask so many questions about these policy and practice questions? It is my sense that no one sits comfortably with whatever decisions we have made because they all have implications and connotations. A serious funder doesn't belittle the impact of one's giving, nor the impact of not giving. Even if one is convinced of the legitimacy of a decision on how to do a cutback in spending, it doesn't diminish the unhappiness.

Thus the Roubini effect in philanthropy. One doesn't need another perfect storm to know how elusive our abilities to accomplish what we did even a year or two ago. One doesn't need to assume only the most dire economic projections to know that people will be un or underemployed for a long time; that expectations for individual careers, retirements, families are being lowered for the foreseeable future; that claims on social services will continue to skyrocket and quality of life arts organizations will suffer even more. Professor Roubini's projections may be off – but he does provide a sober reminder to those of us in this field that we will have several years before we can again rest comfortably that our giving is able to address so many of the needs and causes we believe in.

"If You've Seen One..."
(The Landscape)
- December 31ˢᵗ, 2008 -

One of the first truisms one learns upon entering the foundation field is the old saw: "If you've met one foundation, you've met one foundation." While an exaggeration to be sure, the idiosyncratic nature of foundations is as diverse as the giving patterns, styles and cultures of individual philanthropists and donors. This is not surprising, of course, since most foundations (other than corporate ones) were established by individual donors/philanthropists, their families, their accountants or their trust attorneys. The motivations for establishing them can be tax benefits, family involvement, immortality, or regularizing one's giving when income could vary radically from year to year.

Indeed the character of a foundation is usually established early, when the donor/founder is still involved. But by the third generation, it is very rare for the leadership of a foundation to remain in the hands of volunteer family members (even when they are still involved on the board). By the third generation, variations in motivation, wealth, geography, values, and family commitments typically mean that a family foundation can be a meeting ground but rarely a primary commitment for many within the family. Thus, it is fairly common that, by the third generation, a continuing family foundation will be professionally administered or directed (sometimes by a member of the family designated for that responsibility/honor).

The overwhelming majority of foundations are still controlled by living donors. Only in the last decade have we begun to see a growing number of survivor foundations, which are functioning after the death of the founder. Within the next decade this number will grow and reflect the tremendous (and much discussed) transfer of wealth.

In my work with families and foundations, first and foremost, I must determine who is the client. A foundation where the founder maintains full control and expects it to die shortly after he/she does is really to be treated like a personal giving vehicle. The client is clearly the donor. Recently after I gave a presentation about transferring values across generations and learning how to share decision making, the first comment was made by a community leader who exclaimed: "I don't understand this entire discussion; I made the money and I'll decide how to spend it!" Not surprisingly there was little incentive for others in his family to participate in his "family" foundation.

Sometimes, the donor sincerely does want to involve other generations, but is doubtful that subsequent generations share, or even understand, his or her values. The perception of the founder may indeed be correct, but often, s/he is not. Many times, the other members of a family do share the basic underlying values but differ on how they should be implemented philanthropically. A founder may support healthcare, perhaps by naming a research center or a hospital wing; younger members of the family may be more interested in alternative care or more hands on interventions. A founder may wish to endow an organization to which s/he has a long standing commitment; younger funders may see little value in tying up assets which could do more now, and allow the foundation to respond to new and emerging challenges not anticipated by Mom or Granddad. A founder may wish to limit giving to the community where the family made its wealth; as children and grandchildren disperse, there is little enthusiasm for this kind of restriction. In these cases, the client is the "family." A sensitive and thoughtful advisor can help translate between generations, mediate discussions about legitimate and abiding values, and help initiate a course whereby there is a greater buy-in by and gratification for all family members.

In family foundations of this stage of development, the advisory process differs little from that which applies to a family without a foundation. There is a family culture, a distinct source of wealth, a greater or lesser degree of openness to risk, a desire for or against recognition or anonymity, and a range of priorities, and often the absence of systematic decision making. Jewish community foundations which work with family foundations will be most successful if they themselves have a culture of being donor centered and deal as honest brokers in the advisory process. If a federation foundation policy makes that impossible, it is probably better to invite in an independent philanthropy advisor for some segment of work with this family foundation.

Once a foundation becomes staff directed or administered, the process begins to change. Typically a staff directed foundation has a more formal process of grant application, more formal accountability and reporting expectations, and more defined focus and restrictions. Depending on the foundation, all requests must be reviewed and vetted by professional staff. A well-run foundation has a clear set of deadlines and procedures. There is less likelihood that any individual trustee can determine the outcome of a grant request on a discretionary basis.[6] In the case of staff directed/administered foundations, federations are competitors for annual or special grants. Such foundations will not typically feel a sense of noblesse oblige to umbrella charities such as federations, but may welcome innovative and special project requests. Family foundations at this stage of development are particularly sensitive to a need for grants to be outcome oriented, for grants to reflect the perspectives of the range of board members and to do honor to – but not obeisance to – the legacy of the founder.

---

[6] Many foundations allow board members limited discretionary grantmaking as a way to obviate the pressure on the board to bypass the foundation's mission and focus.

A few comments on so-called "mega-donors" most of whom have established foundations to facilitate their philanthropy. For our purposes, "mega" does NOT necessarily refer to the size of the foundation rather the scope of focus. There are numerous very large donors on the local level whose foundations give more than most of well-known funders who are considered the mega-donors. These local donors' focus is primarily local and responsive to needs and causes in their own back yards. They have chosen not to join in national or international partnerships in which they would find themselves removed from the institutions that are the beneficiaries of their gifts. The mega foundations, on the other hand, typically have a broader vision and mission and see their role as being to address the major communal issues of the day. They may choose to give locally or through federations but these are not their priorities. These funders are most interested in projects that bridge institutional limitations and clearly address cutting edge challenges. Partnerships, multi-institutional collaborations, and innovation are more likely to attract their interest than more traditional kinds of requests. In the case of the mega-foundations where the founder is active, there is typically also a senior executive and well-respected professional staff, although the role and function of these professionals varies widely. The foundations that work best are those where there is a transparent partnership between the foundation funder and the senior professional. Where that is lacking, there is often a challenge to determine "Who's on first?"

It is also appropriate to review the changing nature of corporate foundations. There has always been a delicate balance in the corporate world between using corporate philanthropy to be a good communal citizen vs. serving the marketing needs of the company. In recent years, corporate philanthropy has veered very much toward the marketing end. Among the many reasons are the surfeit of mergers and consolidations, the intense pressure of quarterly earnings, and increased sensitivity to perceived political sensitivities. "Cause related marketing" or "market driven philanthropy" are two of the terms often used. Increasingly, if a project cannot be shown to be of value to the bottom line, it is not of interest to corporate funders. Those seeking funds from corporations should explore both sponsorships and corporate foundations as two separate addresses for support.

A final few comments: foundations are now functioning in a very different climate than existed just a few short years ago. Anyone can view a foundation's 990 and see a complete list of grantees and board members. States attorneys-general are paying close attention to ethical and best practices for grantmaking foundations, the federal government has raised expectations that private foundation philanthropy will step in to replace reduced public funding. And younger funders have mandated that their charitable investments must be justified by measurable returns. Private foundations are no longer the vanity plates of the wealthy, but are serious commitments of the philanthropically inclined. As more and more family foundations come of age in the years to come, it behooves all of us who work with them to be aware of their growing sophistication. Rigor will define their own work and the demands they will make of us.

The Power of Social Networking – And of Funders

- May 21st, 2008 -

L ast week, I attended a session for professional speakers on how to understand and use web-based social networking. For those of us who are, shall we say, chronologically challenged, it was instructive to say the least. I am a member of a bunch of these sites (Facebook, LinkedIn, etc.) but had certainly not figured out how to use them for anything other than curiosity or to respond when someone asked to be my "friend." (How can one say, "No?!") I knew enough that I had to be there, but not quite enough to know what to do when I got there.

In any case, the presenter, whose name I won't give here for reasons that may become obvious later, ended his presentation with a cautionary tale. It is a long and complicated story which would have made a great sit-com and, with a different ending, a wonderful romantic comedy. But real life was less kind. The outlines of this long and complicated story are about a couple who met on a dating site and then in person. They enjoyed each other's company but for peculiar reasons, follow-up contacts went astray. The (wrongly) jilted fellow then sent a bill for half of the cost of the date, and even left such a message on her voice mail.

The offended lass sent a copy of the email and voice mail to the presenter of this story, who took it upon himself to disseminate both to his massive social network. The bottom line of the tale, as he told it, was that the fellow lost his job and had to move to a different city under a new assumed name.

The moral of this story, according to the presenter, of course, was that one should be careful what one says or writes. Fair enough, but what galled me was that the presenter told this story with no shame or embarrassment. He revealed no sense of ethical dilemma in his own behavior. Even if the original guy acted like a jerk, and the woman was justifiably annoyed or hurt, does that justify ruining someone's life? And especially is it justified for a non-offended outside observer to act unilaterally in such a damaging way?

What was equally challenging to me was that I seemed to be the only one there who felt this sense of moral outrage. Was I truly operating on a different ethical standard than the world around me or was I missing something?

So I consulted with my tech guru, someone who was just honored as one of the leading lights of his (younger) generation, known for his expertise in the world of internet design, communication, and networking. He told me that his generation does not believe in a concept of privacy; that all behavior and information is likely to be open to anyone (transparent), so why pretend otherwise. Therefore, the cautionary part of the tale was real. However, he said that there are limits. The absence of privacy does not mean that one can be gratuitously mean and destructive. He, I was reassured, concurred that the presenter overstepped his bounds.

What, you may ask, are the implications for philanthropists? I would say that this illustrates the implied power of the funder, the impact of our behavior – even when unintended. Our words and actions can impact how other funders look upon potential grantees; our comments to and about others carry additional weight because of the power of the dollar sign; our endorsement can leverage – for good, and our rejection can leverage – for naught. We as funders often act as if we are in doing so in vacuum but there is an extended social network that acts upon our signals. The story above was told as a cautionary tale, but its lesson to me is that our actions must always be infused with sensitivity to morality and ethics.

NextGen:
A Flawed Concept For Our Times
But What About Families?

- December 2nd, 2008 -

Let me begin by saying that I really don't like the term *NextGen*. It typically is simply the latest euphemism for "young leadership" or other ways in which established organizations try to entice those perceived to be too young to be true organizational leaders to develop a connection and commitment. Underlying it is a very patronizing concept. It says: you are not rich enough or not proven enough to really be worth listening to. We aren't ready to give you real power but we are hoping that some day you will pay your dues sufficiently that we will invite you to the grown-up table.

From an organizational perspective, this seems to make all the sense in the world: most younger people don't have the means to contribute at a top leadership level, it builds a "bench strength" of volunteers for the time when a space opens up, it allows acculturation into the values and styles of the organization, and builds a tradition of loyalty which should pay future dividends. Every organization knows that the future must include the young(er) folks, so why not cultivate them now? And for some organizations this has been working.

But for too many, this means that superannuated or entrenched leadership simply retains control for an indefinite, perhaps too long, time. It means that the energy, creativity, and innovative thinking of younger people is simply lost or delayed. It means that many younger folk stop waiting and find other, more responsive outlets for their voluntarism.

A few years ago, I spoke to the international leadership of a very prestigious organization. At this retreat, their top "young leadership " was honored. I don't remember everyone, but I do recall that one of the honorees was a 50 year-old retiree, another was a 48 year-old mayor; others were similarly accomplished. Yet without irony, this group bestowed their recognition on these "young" "future" leaders. Old enough and accomplished enough to make a difference in the larger world, not yet ready to sit at the grown-up table for this nonprofit. How many of their peers would have been willing to wait their turn?

My own personal experience was similar: when I moved to NYC to head a significant foundation, I was already into my 50's. Presumably, I had done enough by that time to merit such a position. Yet two international groups invited me to take an active role in their young leadership divisions. I was a bit unsure whether to be insulted or amused. Mirele convinced me that I should consider it a compliment; that I must have looked younger than my chronological age.

The short sightedness is not only that it is depriving the groups of fresh thinking; in many cases it is hastening their irrelevance. Frankly, the world has changed; loyalty is a very rare attribute and there is little evidence that it is rewarded; paying long-term dues is hardly a convincing life plan. After all, there is little evidence that the ruling generations have made judgments that have made the world a better, kinder, gentler, more caring place than it would be in the hands and minds of a younger generation. The most exciting philanthropy, arts, political phenomena are surely not emerging from entrenched institutions but from those on the outside.

Not every new idea, project, approach, innovation is great, or worthy of success. Lots fail and many deserve to fail. But so what? So many of the ideas are successful and deserving. So many new ideas in philanthropy are emerging from younger folks, perhaps in need of some seasoning but asking the right questions, proposing credible solutions, and engaging entire swaths of the population in redressing the inequities in a flawed world. *NextGen*? It seems to me that it is truer to say *ThisGen*. Most nonprofits would do well to learn from them. And younger folks should realize it is already their world. They shouldn't wait for a place at the table. Set your own.

Of course, all of these changes have an impact and implication for my own work. But there is one piece of specific concern to many families who have experienced or intuited these changes: how and when to integrate this new thinking into family giving strategies. It is surely not a new question to wonder when and how to bring younger folk into a family foundation or decision-making. But what if the newer generations simply see the world differently? Have a very different understanding of the roles of philanthropy and the nonprofit sector? Have a very different instinct regarding why philanthropy and how it can make a difference? In these cases, the challenge is not how to bring children, grandchildren, great grandchildren into the inner circle in a thoughtful and systematic way; it is to recognize that the worldview represented by some of these generations is so different that it challenges the very way in which family philanthropy functions.

In my work, this is one of the most intriguing and interesting challenges, sometimes leading to wonderful intergenerational understanding and visionary philanthropic responses; most often leading to a respectful and functional mutual acceptance; occasionally to a nonresolvable inability to reach a mutually satisfying philanthropic strategy. For these last, *NextGen* may be exactly the right term.

The Case for Perpetuity

J ulius Rosenwald, an often forgotten but visionary philanthropist of the last century, believed
deeply that his philanthropic dollars should be
distributed during his lifetime. He wanted his vast
wealth, much of it designated toward charitable and
philanthropic endeavors, to be used to solve the problems he saw, not to be held in trust in perpetuity to be
distributed by future generations. Let others, he explic-
itly argued, solve the problems of their times, with their
means.

Over the past year, there has been much noise, and
some rare clarity of voice, in public discourse regarding
the role of philanthropy in the public weal. Much of this
debate has centered on the wisdom or legitimacy of establishing endowments or foundations in perpetuity, and
a surprising amount of that has come, in my experience
from younger funders.

It hasn't been the best of times for the philanthropic
community. It has proven itself every bit as susceptible
to guile, avarice, and self-importance as the business
community.[7]

To make matters worse, these affronts and abuses
have come at a time of tremendous challenges to philanthropic resources. Despite the profound gains in last
year's market, it is a rare foundation or major funder

---

[7] Perhaps not so surprising since most philanthropic foundations
have as their base, resources from individuals who have made
those fortunes in the business world, and are typically governed
by those same people and their families and close advisors. I
don't know how extensive abuse of public trust will prove to have
been in the business community; I suspect that, in the philanthropic community, it will be shown that the good far exceeds the
rotten.

with the dispensable income of two or three years ago. History tells us that, even with a rebound in the economy, the philanthropic enterprise will trail the economy by two or three years.

The challenge is compounded yet further by the government's recent attention to philanthropy. Not surprising if one thinks about it. After all, our national debt has exploded at the cost of human services. Where might one find relief? One has the sense that politicians are viewing foundations with a Willie Sutton perspective; that's where the money is. If one has exempted the wealthiest individuals, beneficiaries of tremendous tax relief and the most immediate beneficiaries of an economic rebound, philanthropic foundations, donor advised funds, and the like are a repository of substantial and enticing dollars. Why not shift the burden of responsibility for human need to those quasi private and now suspect institutions? Why allow a permanent endowment?

I am troubled by this political and expedient approach rather than a more conceptual and thoughtful concern with the proper role of philanthropy in American society. But not surprised.

I have been surprised, though, by what I have heard from younger funders. Their abiding skepticism toward large and bureaucratic institutions is joined by an altogether new vision: that of free market philanthropy. This approach argues that endowments "soften" the drive of not-for-profit organizations. This argument says that each organization should be forced to make its case in the only measure that makes sense, in the fund raising sphere. Endowments allow organizations to be less agile, responsive, entrepreneurial, or customer oriented. If an organization cannot make its case among funders, it should cease and let others who can step forward. After all, they say, that is what makes for vibrancy and vitality, with the funder being ultimate arbiter of success.

Why am I troubled? Any of us who have been on the funding side know that there are organizations which have long outlived their usefulness and are being kept alive by carefully nurtured reserves. Moreover, we all know organizations that have lost their way because their funders and endowments continue to keep them going for sentimental reasons and not because of the vitality of their missions. And we all know bloated bureaucratic institutions for which it would be virtually impossible to measure any outcome other than how much money they raised. And, regrettably, we know too many organizations that patronize their so-called "young leaders" but rarely have space at the table for them to become true shapers of the organization. There is much empirical evidence to justify the cynicism and skepticism I have heard from those of a younger generation.

But, I am still not fully persuaded by them. When, earlier in my career, I had executive responsibilities for organizations dependent on donors, I saw the shortsightedness of buildings that were crumbling because there was no endowment. What donor would want to have his or her name associated with an organization that couldn't maintain its infrastructure, or properly honor the wishes of donors of a previous generation?

More, I saw the difficulty of developing a reliable and responsive system when funding was dependent on the whims of donors and the faddishness of causes. Human services, cultural accomplishment, and educational excellence are not achieved in the blink of an eye, and are not often most effectively produced by popularity contests.

It is too easy to look at several large not-for-profit organizations and see them as the norm. But of the over 1.2 million not-for-profits in the United States, few are universities or United Ways. The overwhelming majority are small, local, special interest organizations. They often have tiny staff and very little access to meaningful capital. They live hand to mouth, or donor to donor. But they are often cutting edge, creative, and ahead of the popularity curve. Were it not for endowed foundations that have the expertise to see beyond raw percentages and beyond slick marketing, many of the most innovative and responsive ideas would never emerge, or serve very local communities.

There are good and justifiable reasons for a funder, family, foundation, or philanthropist to choose to limit their beneficence to a specific time frame. There are good motivations for doing so, and among my clients there are many who have made that choice.

But there are also good and valid reasons for endowments and foundations to be established with an eye toward perpetuity. Not all current problems lend themselves to immediate solutions; not all funding should be based on effective marketing; popularity is not the same as values; donors with clearly articulated values may want to help guarantee the implementation of those values long after they are gone; foundations with clearly articulated values can transcend the whims of the moment. Without society's risk capital, the best ideas may never see the light of day.

Any of us who have been on the grant making side know that nothing about the future can be guaranteed. An endowment can enhance but cannot guarantee the likelihood that future professionals will bring credit and honor to a donor. Current spending can enhance but cannot guarantee that a particular need will be fulfilled or a project will achieve its goals. Not-for-profit organizations need to earn the trust of those who will invest in their ideas and ideals. But funders need to be encouraged to recognize the validity and legitimacy of both kinds of funding.

Philanthropy has the uniqueness of being able to think the big thoughts, and address the long-term. I have learned much from my students and younger clients. I would hope that one of the lessons they will learn is to see the validity of those gifts that address tomorrow's tomorrow.

Welcome to Our Field, Mr. Ubinas

- August 14ᵗʰ, 2007 -

C ongratulations on your appointment as the new president of the prestigious and influential Ford Foundation. You have accepted the assignment at a very propitious moment in the world of philanthropy and public policy. Rarely has there been a convergence of so many factors challenging the value of values and the worth of wealth in American society. The Ford Foundation has a noteworthy history in helping to define the agenda and pushing the envelope (pardon the clichés). It appears that your personal background and perhaps even your professional one will give you a distinctive perspective on many of these issues. Those of us in the field extend our collegial hand and wish you much success has you move into this sector.

If I have any ambivalence about your appointment, it is not about you but your background. Once again, a nonprofit has celebrated that it has reached beyond the predictable to select a leader. I am a big believer in career change and that one shouldn't be bound for a lifetime in a narrow niche; transferability should become a norm in our society. It allows growth and vitality and indeed productivity at various stages of life. Why should a decision made at age 20 or even 30 or 40 limit our willingness to change as our life experiences expand and our interests mature. So your change from McKinsey to Ford is to be applauded.

What concerns me, though, is that one can hardly imagine the reverse happening. Can you imagine Citicorp proudly celebrating that it has selected a United Way executive as its next President? Can one conceive that a hospital president becomes the next CEO of Federated? Nonprofit boards take pride that they have enticed an employee of the private sector. Implicit is that a newly appointed executive must be better at what they do or know or can accomplish because they have succeeded in the private, for-profit sector. What does that say to those who have committed themselves to careers in the nonprofit sector? That as good as they are they will never be considered as good as someone who has chosen another sector? That if they were really that good, they would have chosen (or have been chosen by) the private sector? That they would have made money instead of meaning?

Many readers might know something about my own professional journey. In 1968, when I first started my career, I chose to work on campuses. In 1968 I was the envy of everyone I knew; it was where the action was - where real expression could take place. When I chose to leave that part of my career in 1982, the prevailing attitudes were quite different. People would say to me, "You are a smart guy; why aren't you in a job where you could be making money?" "You work too hard to be in the nonprofit sector." Envy had morphed into puzzlement at my questionable career judgment.

Why my riff at this time? Because in the work I do, I frequently hear that funders need to make sure that private sector thinking must be brought to bear to the work of nonprofits. Staff appointments are only the visible tip of this thinking. Efficiency and measurable outcomes are more likely to be the defined goals of a grant than solving real human need.. Disrespect for overburdened and under-rewarded staff is more likely to be heard than a commitment to make the necessary changes to entice the very best to this sector or to retain capable staff.

The Ford Foundation, Mr. Ubinas, is an opinion shaper, a multiplier, as the Germans would call it. It is crucial that, as you join this sector, you underscore your commitment to the distinctiveness and unique contributions of the nonprofit world to the weal of our world. Make no mistake: I am not advocating mediocrity, inefficiency, or irrelevance. I am hoping that you help lead the way so that, as we redress those deficiencies, we don't punish the victims of years of neglect. This sector needs your success; we welcome you.

The Sound of One Shoe Dropping

- May 29th, 2008 -

T he not-for-profit world has, in the United States, always occupied an uneasy tension with the government. In a country that has great ambivalence about the appropriateness of government providing basic human services, it isn't surprising that a variety of tax preferences exist on the federal, state, and local level for this sector. Yet it has always been uneasy for 2 reasons- one practical and one theoretical.

The practical is obvious. Non-profits still have access to fire, police, sanitation services and other support systems that taxes pay for. It is one thing to exempt non-profits from taxation on their income; it is quite another to say that this exemption applies to public services used by those nonprofits. There are many types of resolution to this question, and it is guaranteed that it will be an even more pressing matter during these next few years of shortfalls in income to municipal coffers.

The conceptual one is more challenging and is suggested by the case referred to in this article: Does the nonprofit sector exist to provide for those in financial need or to provide for needs of the society as they deem interesting or appropriate. If the former, one could make the case that the only museum that deserves to be tax exempt is one which has a need based admission fee. In the case here, we see that a school was held to that standard in a fairly stark and sobering way.

Most of us implicitly believe in a more expansive role of private philanthropy, and the tax code seems to bear that out. It doesn't now (yet) require that one's contribution is justified because of the objectivity of the need, only that the recipient organization is doing something in the public interest in a not-for-profit way. But as the title of the article suggests, I don't think that this is a resolved issue for many and is very likely to be on our communal agenda for quite a while. This Minnesota case may simply be the beginning.

I always appreciate calls from the press since they help me focus my thoughts on issues I have been meaning to write about. This time the inquiry regarded the recent Minnesota decision to remove real estate tax exemption from a day care center.

I don't know any more specifics about this than what I read in *The NY Times*, so these comments are more about the general issue. Some thoughts.[8]

1. The issue of real estate exemption is not a new one. Since non-profit organizations are typically among the largest employers and landowners in any community, the question has arisen in lots of places for a long time. The typical resolution has been for the largest non-profits to make "in lieu of" payments to the municipality for services provided. This has kept the question of tax exemption at bay, but not very far below the surface.

2. Our tax system does not distinguish the relative value of different kinds of non-profit organizations. A contribution to Harvard with its $35 billion endowment counts as much as a contribution to a neighborhood soup kitchen. Much to be said about this, on all sides, but the current facts are, that we do not have to meet an objective means test of relative need to take our deductions.

---

8 Abbreviated to stimulate discussion. I would be happy to expand on any of these at the drop of a hat.

3.   The current national administration has been in power for seven years. Their policy is that there is no such thing as a good tax. Minnesota is probably an example of trickle down economics. As human service support has been cut along with jobs and the economy; municipalities look wherever they can. Those of you who have heard me speak know my feelings about our current policies; suffice it to say that we are seeing the inevitable results.

4.   Funders are not exempt from some culpability. There was a time when funders saw their responsibility to cover deficits of organizations providing needed services. Today, funders downgrade organizations with regular deficits and rank those with "surpluses" and multiple income sources more highly. (Except for the technicality of who gets to keep it, is there really a difference between a profit and a surplus?) In any case, if funders put pressure on the non-profits to maximize income sources, it is not a very big step to have tax authorities ask what business they really are in. Funders are not wrong to want to fund stable, well-run institutions but we should think seriously about the implications of the implicit pressure it puts on those very organizations.

5.   The increasing use of hybrid language and funding models. Funders increasingly "invest" with "nonprofit partners." We conceptualize hybrid models that can provide returns to individuals while also creating tax-exempt structures. We assume that a for-profit solution is probably better than a non-profit solution for health care, environment, etc. We decry inefficiencies at the same time

that we put pressure on their staff overhead (if one cannot afford long time and well trained staff, how does one achieve true effectiveness?) If all this is true, it is a small step to questioning the very value of the nonprofit sector, and therefore, why not put the onus on that sector to justify their service to society. Surely the argument that because there is a flat user fee rather than need based user fees, the nonprofit is essentially not providing nonprofit services is flawed on its face, but it is the kind of argument one will hear if one is not careful with language and values.

I don't think we have heard the last of this issue. After all, municipalities will follow the money wherever it may be, and alas, as we will increasingly see, wherever it may not be. Is it the first or the second shoe?

The Community was Traumatized

- December 22, 2008 -

The community was traumatized – they had managed to absorb political reversals, terrorism, and general economic deterioration. As difficult, upsetting, disconcerting, and challenging each of this succession of crises had been, they had always been by outsiders. This crisis was of a different sort altogether. A powerful insider in the financial community had been indicted; his financial institution bankrupt; huge sums had been lost by individuals and by institutions. This was too close; it cut too deep, it belied trust and loyalty; it was nothing less than a trauma.

No, this was not about a Mr. Madoff, and the country was not the United States. This is the story of Argentina and the story of the phone call we received.

"How quickly can you and Mirele come here?" the caller asked. "We need you." Flattered but puzzled, I asked how I could help. "Because," he said, "our community is in deep emotional depression and anomie; it goes beyond the finances, and deep into the sense of confidence in the future." "Why us?" I replied. "Because, when you were here before, we heard your message. You saw things about our potential that we didn't understand ourselves. You saw that the greatest resources are human, not fiscal. You taught us that we have a depth of knowledge, competence, and creativity to not only emerge from this but to evolve into something newer and better."[9]

We went, and for ten days we spoke everywhere; to young adults, established groups, leadership, and university classes. We spoke early and often. Our message was

---

[9] Okay – maybe not exactly those words, but pretty close.

exactly what we were asked to preach. It wasn't hard since we sincerely do believe that human resources matter more than financial resources to the inherent and long-term health of a society. History has many examples of economically thriving but morally, ethically, or culturally bankrupt places. And those economic riches are usually more transient than societies that believe in people, values, and future.

Now, let us be fair; this is not a case for the suffering servant view of history. Poverty is not a desired end nor is human need a public policy desideratum. But it is an important corrective to the times we are now in to remember that what makes us successful is accomplishment, not avarice; what makes us gratified is achievement, not greed; what makes us proud is altruism not hubris; what makes us smile is many small, daily acts of grace, not one grandiloquent gesture; what makes us wise is that we continue to learn, not that we already know; what gives us a future is that we believe that there is more to do, not more to have.

America is a wealthier country, even as we enter the deepest recesses of this recession, than Argentina was at its depths, and certainly more than America was in the 30's. It is civil society, transparency, decency, humility of place and a commitment to humankind that will see us, and the rest of the world, through this time. Disillusionment is real; disappointment, understandable; anxiety, more than justified. But nihilism and defeatism will yield only that. And the society, and true philanthropy that must emerge from these times cannot be allowed to sink to the depths of despair.

We were simple small voices in our visit to Argentina those years ago; perhaps we brought a message of hope to some few. But the words we shared then are no less real for this time and for our place.

"Change" is a condition; "hope" is an emotion; "commitment" is what will get us there.

How could they not have known?
Perhaps my final Madoff post
- January 8th, 2009 -

As readers of this site are well aware, much of my professional time is spent working with families on matters relating to their philanthropy. It is an extraordinary moment: families invite me in to deal with many matters relating to their deepest values, philanthropic and charitable decisions, questions of when to bring new generations into the formal process, and, indeed, who should be included among the eligible.

In most of these cases, it is a glimpse into a family with the most sincere and genuine motivations, trying to address their own legacy and privilege in a responsible and planful way. The typical family balances the interests of the founder to influence (sometimes control) his or her children and grandchildren with recognition that subsequent generations have different styles, often live in different places, and frequently have different values than the founder. The most typical case is where they really do want this to work, and want my outside experienced facilitation to help them get to a place that both works and feels right.

Sometimes, there is a different agenda on the part of the founder: to resolve family issues through philanthropy. Rarely can or does that work. All of us who are in this field know that, while philanthropy can reinforce family feelings and foster collaboration, it can never resolve unresolved family issues. Sometimes those issues are issues between siblings; sometimes attitudes toward a parent; sometimes it is simply ambivalence or even unhappiness about growing up in a privileged environment, limiting the ability of a child or grandchild to knowing whether their worth is based on finances or character.

One of the questions I am frequently asked about *l'affaire Madoff* is my instinct about who else knew. Many are quite convinced that his sons had to have been involved and that Bernie is taking the heat for them, a last, perhaps desperate noble act.

Maybe. But if my own professional experience is indicative, I wouldn't be so quick to jump to that conclusion. Over the years of working with families, I have worked with many who simply never knew that there was a foundation until the death of the founder, or that they would be appointed to the family foundation board, or had any idea what the family resources were or the scope of those resources. Some families are so open with one another that they find this incomprehensible; others fully recognize this condition: that part of the family culture is mystery about money. It simply is not a legitimate topic for discussion.[10]

There are many reasons for this reticence. Ambivalence about money itself, disbelief that it is real, deep distrust in what others in the family really think about their fellow family members, control... Sometimes, I suspect, it is based on embarrassment about where the money was made and a reluctance to taint a legacy cleansed through generous philanthropic behavior.

When a family finds me, it signifies that some of this, perhaps all of this is now open, or at least under consideration. Second generations try to figure out what Dad or Mom meant (donor intent), but often had lived much of their lives in the shadow of a powerful personality. Third and fourth generations have different emotional attachments or detachments, but their philanthropy is more motivated by their own interests and styles, and the challenge is to correlate it with other family interests. And even the founder may have decided that it is better to

---

[10] Full disclosure: my own upbringing was like that.

influence while alive than rule from the grave. What distinguishes the successful engagement of these issues and more is the sharing of information (all, some, enough...).

Sometime soon we will know who really did or didn't conspire with Bernie Madoff, who was or wasn't culpable for knowingly turning their eyes away, who should have or couldn't have made better judgments, and who were indirect but nevertheless real victims.[11] Given my own professional experience with families, we should withhold judgment on the Madoff sons until we know a lot more.

---

[11] Another full disclosure: that includes us.

Advocacy Funding –
A Surprising & Challenging Response

- August 21ˢᵗ, 2006 -

Perhaps I shouldn't have been surprised... but I was.

It was in an advanced strategic grantmaking seminar at NYU; the subject, "environmental funding..." The guest presenter was emphasizing how most funders with a focus on the environment typically turn toward advocacy projects since so many environmental problems can only be solved by changing issues of the environment depend on public policy and motivating governments to get involved. There is a limit to what individual and grassroots funding can accomplish unless accompanied by action on the part of governments. Our guest presenter spoke of the larger commitment to reinforce and implement. He gave numerous examples of effective advocacy funding and of organizations that have used that funding to achieve with genuine impact.

Our guest's recommendations certainly rang true for me. In my work advising funders with public policy interests, and as a board member, sitting on two grantmaking organizations with missions to reduce anti-hunger and increase co-existence respectively, I have observed a marked predilection by board members for funding organizations with an advocacy commitment. These funders, after all, have learned that, without addressing systemic and endemic issues, all of the on-the-ground efforts will be like tilting at windmills. Although small grants to many food pantries can feed a lot of people, a miniscule change, for example, in the federal budget allocation can feed many more. As a result of my experiences on these boards, I have become convinced of the wisdom of committing funds to the centrality of thoughtful advocacy as an indispensable component of a balanced funding strategy.[12]

The participants in this seminar were not novices in the funding world. As funders themselves or foundation professionals, they had all been challenged with establishing funding priorities and strategies. If you had asked me, I would have assumed that the presenter would find an immediate resonance, and that a receptive audience would be receptive to our guest's recommendations about advocacy funding. I expected that they would find his advice useful, and immediately embrace his recommendations for enhancing the sophistication of their funding strategies. I expected that they would understand how his recommendations could help them to achieve the missions, and in providing a methodology which would allow more effective achievement of their foundations' missions. But that was not the case.

In fact, the reaction of the participants in the seminar was quite the opposite. To my surprise, they challenged our guest. They asked him why anyone would want to assume that there was either the will or willingness of the government to respond adequately and efficiently to human needs. And, even if there were the will, after watching the response to such catastrophes as Katrina in the Gulf Coast, they asked, can we as funders truly believe that government spending is as effective as support for local on the ground organizations? These organizations which know who is suffering, who is homeless, who is jobless and who is missing? A local church or non-profit may be limited in its scope, but it is thorough in its commitment to rebuild a house, or provide clothing, and offer counseling.

---

[12] Of course, there is also a need to support those local food pantries. But as well, without supportive pubic policy, there will never be a reduction in the number of hungry children.

Furthermore, the participants argued, Katrina was hardly an isolated incident. They pointed to the significant reduction in government human service funding, and the increased reliance on voluntary support for vulnerable populations. In this environment, they perceive that direct dollars given to support direct services surely achieve more than dollars directed toward indirect and, to their mind, dubious advocacy for changes in government policies.

A rebuttal to these arguments isn't hard to make. The very scale of need for human services outweighs the ability of any non-profit to replace government funding. For example, in the Gulf Coast alone, there was a need for 250,000 homes. The largest number of homes that Habitat for Humanity had ever built before Katrina was 5,000 per year! And Habitat is by far the largest non-profit homebuilder in the nation. Only government has the potential to build enough houses to house Katrina's homeless.

Similarly, before Buffett's recent gift, the pre-Buffett Gates Foundation's assets were approximately $33 billion. A 5% payout on these assets yields a massive $1.65 billion per year. However, this massive amount is dwarfed by the National Institute of Health's annual budget of $28 billion. Gates can do a lot of global health, but it can never do what government can do. Like numbers can be demonstrated in an entire range of human service and educational areas.

The purpose of these comments, and in raising this issue in my seminar is not political. Caring and thoughtful people can most assuredly disagree about the proper roles of government and private philanthropy. The point I want to make is about how the conversation among the participants in my seminar illustrates the impact of larger societal attitudes, which in turn influences how we choose to spend our charitable funds. As I thought more about the attitudes of the participants in my seminar, I realized that I should not have been surprised. Attitudes toward government are just one of the factors that have led to marked changes in the funding environment over the past few years. These changes include the emphasis on: outcome and impact measures, increases in restricted and targeted giving, suspicion about the effectiveness of giving to umbrella charities, more reliance on private sector benchmarks, and increased interest on the part of funders for a hands-on relationship with grantees.

While all of these changes have contributed to more effective philanthropy, we must temper our embrace of the attitudes that they represent. We should not let skepticism slide into cynicism because we risk allowing philanthropy to suffer from the myopia of the dubious. Recent real and publicized abuses in the voluntary sector, on both the funding and non profit sides of the table, should not shake our confidence in the integrity of the majority of people engaged in the voluntary sector. We must insist that our funding dollars be spent with care, but we must also be careful not to allow ourselves to confuse efficiency with effectiveness in how we evaluate our grantees.

Although it is tempting to give our money only to direct service programs where we can see and feel that we are making a difference, we need to resist the urge to do so. One might well make the case that this is precisely the moment when funding for advocacy is most needed. Careful and thoughtful philanthropy allows a perspective and objectivity which can inform the public discourse and serve as a valuable perspective, and can prod the public sector to do that which only it can do. We must stop and give serious pause before we surrender the unique role of philanthropy as the risk capital of society. We must resist the pressure to accept the idea that private philanthropy can somehow replace a public commitment by the public at large to meeting human needs through the collective efforts of government.

Our challenge, of course, is how best to fulfill the missions of our foundations. Do we do best by funding immediate needs, with visible results? Sometimes it is indirectly, by funding advocacy? Or do we do so in more indirect means, through on the ground experts and policy advocacy. The answer will differ for each funder and each foundation, and even for each issue. But one would hope that every decision we make will be informed by a judicious judgment of which kind of funding is best suited to the best long-term results, and not primarily by our skepticism about our government's commitment to the greater social good.

The One-Sided Table [13]

- *Winter 2006* -

D iplomatic negotiations start with the shape of the table: Who sits where, how many get to sit there, and, as important, who doesn't get close. It is often the creativity in shaping the discourse that determines the likelihood of success. The same is true in our world. This is a story about the shapes that define the philanthropy community table.

The Two-Sided Table

The first communal table at which I sat had two sides. It had space for those who needed money and those who had it. The side of the table representing or facilitating or planning or convening or coordinating those who had money was typically the umbrella system, represented by such groups as United Way or Jewish Federations or Catholic Charities or other re-granting agencies. In my case, earlier in my career, my primary concern was the other side: to advocate for enhanced support for undercapitalized, underfunded, and under-recognized institutions and priorities.

The early 90's were the heady days for those of us in the educational/identity world. For lots of us, we got our start in the late 60's, but our message was only fully recognized in the early 90's. The endorsement of the indispensability of education and other "continuity" programs led to increases in funding and a new focus. It was a confluence of other factors as well: optimism about the state

---

13 A somewhat different version of this essay was published in *CONTACT*.

of the world following the end of the cold war, the peace dividend which led to a booming economy, the coming to power of the "boomer" generation, and the earliest suggestions of the transformative nature of technology all allowed issues of the future to take center stage. As it happens, the big umbrella funding systems gradually changed from being the central convener to more, shall we say, monopolistic or controlling. It was their dollars and those affluent philanthropists and business people whom they brought to the table which made it possible for programs which addressed committed identity and education to move from institutional poverty to bourgeois credibility.

The Three-Sided Table

In the 90's the table developed a different shape. By this time, I was exclusively on the side of the funders. I discovered that there are funders who didn't have any interest in seeing the United Way type systems serve as a conduit or vetting agency for their philanthropic dollars. They viewed the "consensus" and "deliberative" process valued by the umbrella/intermediary system to be incrementalism. If it were true that the community was quickly eroding, a marginal re-adjustment of funding priorities would not solve the problem. The very word "continuity" as used by the federations became a symbol of a system that didn't deliver the goods. These funders began to sit at the table, on their own, next to the federations and across from the grantees, and directed their own funds, directly, to the causes and institutions they felt reflected their own priorities.

The One-Sided Table

The 3-sided approach was of limited satisfaction to independent funders. By the mid-90's, philanthropists began to bring a new, fertile and challenging approach to their funding of the "future." Free standing partnerships, collaborations, and venture philanthropy projects emerged in rapid succession. With some degree of lip service to the federation role, mega and not so mega funders began to do their own things. While each of these efforts, many of which I had the privilege of being involved with in their early days, has had its own history, strengths and weaknesses, goals and challenges, destiny and destination, all of them have been characterized by several factors which challenged communal norms:

1. They were well funded enough to make noise.

2. They had enough "clout" for that noise to be listened to.

3. They were about impacting masses of people...

4. ... in record time

5. They were self-funded by philanthropists and governed by boards comprised of the funders or their staff representatives.

Through partnerships, collaborations, and venture philanthropy projects, philanthropists have attempted to reinvent the very structure of the funding world. Nothing less than a radical transformation would stand a chance with the millions who found that the non-profit enterprise had become soporific, self absorbed, irrelevant, and alienating. As the newly-coronated world philosopher Bono recently put it, "It has to feel like history; incrementalism puts the audience in a snooze." He might well have been sitting at the one-sided table with these philanthropists.

The Outside of the Table

Recently, I have been a part of the world not typically at the table. I have been teaching philanthropists and foundation professionals from all facets of American life, and advising families and foundations from all over. I have gained a new perspective on these developments within. For all of our innovative instincts, we did not invent partnerships, venture projects, or the goal of using funds to change communal behaviors. There are lessons to be learned on how to do it right.

What have I have learned from the world beyond our many sided tables? I have learned that venture projects without "exit strategies" from the beginning often doom well-meaning and promising projects; that disaster funding without plans for long-term systemic change is self indulgent and often disappointing; that there are fads in philanthropy, and "new" is often exciting, but the new may or may not be better than that which was tested over time; that partnerships can allow a creative leveraging of limited resources, but they can also be safe, prestigious ways of avoiding the hard questions of risk; that the community may be better off with a room full of various shaped tables than aspire to only one shape or size.

I have also learned that real change comes from learning, and learning comes from humility, an all too elusive commodity. "Making a difference" implies meaningful change, and change carries with it the risk of failure. Only those funders willing to risk, whether in types of funding or in scope of grantees, and to learn from those risks, will precipitate the transformational, adaptable, agile, vibrant and robust 21st Century community that they hope will define their legacies.

Chapter Three:

Philanthropy in a Time of Crisis

I n good times, it may not be easy to know whom to give gifts, why, and which gifts make the most impact. But most funders view giving in good times as an expression of what matters most to them, a reflection of their subjective interest. Objective need may inform their thinking, but decisions are invariably based on what they personally (or the trustees of a foundation) care about.

In time of crisis or profound need, the conversation plot thickens. Should one suspend one's normal priorities, interests, or procedures because there are needs that supersede those, at least for a short time? We certainly saw that behavior after 9/11 and hurricane Katrina. But in the overwhelming number of cases, funders quickly resumed their previous funding strategies.

What about the current financial crisis, which will certainly be more pervasive and longer lasting than either 9/11 or Katrina. Should there be a new imperative or is this exactly the time when a careful funder holds steady?

It is useful to recall that the last massive economic dislocation led to the current philanthropic pattern. One of the unintended consequences of the New Deal, Social Security, and the concept of the safety net was that it allowed the shift in private philanthropy from "objective need" to "subjective interest." Before the 1930's, everyone except the very rich knew that, without their personal giving, there was no other place to turn. The only safety nets were those provided by charitable giving. But when the society established a safety net, however porous it may still be, it freed us to think about what mattered to us as individuals, not only what those in need may need. I suspect that the next several years will yield another shift in our understanding of the role of private philanthropy and public policy.

This economic crisis hit a symbolic nadir at the end of 2008. The Madoff scandal was not only the story of a massive Ponzi scheme, but also, more to our point, it impacted many foundations and nonprofits in shocking and embarrassing ways. The press has been endlessly fascinated; nothing in my career has led to more quotes and interviews. A number of essays in this chapter speak to the issues that emerge from this sad, sad story.

The Real Problem Has Been Arrogance, Not Greed
- May 31ˢᵗ, 2009 -

Today's New York Times reported that both Harvard and Columbia had instituted variations on a theme: an ethics oath for newly minted MBA graduates. It appears that Harvard's is more voluntary but also requires a pro-active step; Columbia's is built into the honors code and is assumed to apply for the entire career yet to be for all in the Columbia B-School orbit.

The article seemed to suggest that ethically driven financial wizards would restrain their greed for the greater good – because of the power of an oath. It is a well-meaning and timely initiative. Who can criticize the welcome introduction of an ethics mandate in a curriculum committed to learning all the effective, efficient, innovative, and emerging ways to make money? Surely....

Teaching ethics is a necessary but insufficient way to imbue good behavior. Over 30 years ago, I taught some seminars in medical ethics at a medical school. They were well received and the discussions were lively and sincere. I am told that such courses and seminars are even more prevalent today. Yet, I regret to say, that over the years, I have come across a number of doctors for whom that thinking was left at the academy gates. When challenged, they had plenty of exculpatory explanations, but it was clear that, when it might have mattered most, ethics was the furthest thing from their mind. Were it not for laws and regulations, one wonders how internalized these ethics issues would be.

To return to our issue, I am one who believes that greed was not the driving force that led to the dismantling of the world financial order over the last 18 months. Greed isn't new; it is not that many steps removed from attributes we respect such as ambition and drive. I am not at all persuaded that the Wall Street and hedge fund hotshots of the last era were greedier than their predecessors, or of most others not in the industry.

I do believe though that there has been a more perverse dilemma characteristic of the era we are concluding: and that is arrogance. Greed is having personal interest beyond reasonable expectation, even at the expense of others. Arrogance is that the rules don't even apply, that one is above or beyond them.

How else to explain the push to dismantle regulation? How else to explain financial advisors who sit on nonprofit boards and push investments to their own firms, feeling that conflict of interest or prudent investor rules can be by-passed? How else to explain a sense of entitlement regardless of impact on others or even proven results?

We still have rules and used to have even more to limit greed; but arrogance defies easy legislative fixes. One hopes that the corrective of lost pride, wealth, and credibility will do what best practices and rules didn't – bring a sense of propriety, humility, and balance to the next era. But to do so will require more than ethics oaths. If one doesn't believe rules apply, what does an honor code mean? It will require a social expectation that judges such behavior, and boards that insist that they indeed do have a higher calling.

Some years ago, I had lunch at a famous restaurant with the scion of the wealthy family that had part ownership of this destination dining spot. There was a dress code for men – sport jackets or suits required. The scion chose to come in a dress t-shirt. The maître d quietly offered a jacket kept for such occasions. My young luncheon companion politely declined the offer – and then commented to me after the maître d was out of earshot.

He confided, "Ownership should have its privileges." Sitting there, I could imagine his father responding more emphatically, and with not a little bit of pique, "No, ownership should have its responsibilities!"

Ethics knows that there are rules; responsibility is knowing the difference.

Philanthropy's Response to the Current Financial Crisis
- October 12th, 2008 -

E arlier this week, we formally announced that the program teaching funders, philanthropists, and grantmakers at New York University would henceforth be known as the *Academy for Grant-making and Funder Education*. While we have proudly taught hundreds of individual funders and professionals in the field over the past 7 years, this new name will allow folks to find us and to more readily identify this focus of the *Center for Philanthropy*. It is a welcome development about which I am quite pleased.

At the luncheon announcing the *Academy*, the keynote speaker was Jack Rosenthal, the very respected and thoughtful head of *The New York Times Foundation*. His remarks, and those of a respondent from the non-profit field, Ariel Zwang of *Safe Horizons*, stimulated a very energetic and often impassioned conversation. These thoughts are in response to what seemed to be emerging "orthodoxies" about philanthropic behavior in the current financial free fall.

Idea #1

Philanthropy's values are ego-driven and not needs-driven. One speaker bemoaned was how much easier it is to raise $200 million for a museum than $1 million for a soup kitchen.

Idea #2

It is inherently wrong that only 5-10% of philanthropic giving is specifically targeted to serving the needs of the poor.

Idea #3

Funders don't coordinate their work, so that there is needless duplication and inefficiency in grant-making.

Idea #4

Private philanthropy should step up to the plate to replace government cutbacks.

Idea #5

Funders are unhelpful to grantees in times of change, especially in providing appropriate technical assistance in arranging orderly and strategic cutbacks.

Each of these has a good deal of truth but taken together distort the appropriate and proper role of philanthropy. Especially at times when everyone has less to give or spend, we have to balance our response to short-term needs with long-term strategies, so these comments are meant to stand as correctives to the emerging pressures on funders. None of us should be insensitive to real human needs and unresponsive to profoundly challenging moments. But it is also important to remember that private philanthropy cannot and should not be expected to be the solution to major societal issues.

It is important to remember that in the face of hunger, we can all support soup kitchens and pantries. But all of that support pales in the face of what an expansion of the food stamp program can do. We are naïve to believe that our own private generosity can feed millions of people over months. Only a national system like the food stamp program can. Direct service funding for food, a perfectly fine thing to do, without a concomitant commitment to advocate for effective public policy, a necessary thing to do, is inefficient philanthropy.

Similarly, coordination of private funding during times of disaster was raised. Who can argue against the validity of better coordination among funders and service deliverers – especially at times of crisis. But, the question remains: whose ultimate responsibility should it be to respond to disasters? Shouldn't the demand be to rebuild a credible FEMA? Shouldn't the role of private philanthropy be to build beyond the role of what FEMA can provide – long-term, targeted responses, not to replace short-term interventions, a proper government function.

One participant mentioned the extraordinary consolidation of wealth in endowments at places like Harvard. Isn't there something wrong with such hoarding? Probably. But let us remember that even if university endowments were mandated to spend at the same rate as private foundations, they wouldn't come close to replacing the cutbacks in Pell Grants – the single most significant source of support for higher education for the middle class.

What is at stake in this discourse, passionately and sympathetically raised among many thoughtful folks in the philanthropy world, who are wringing their proverbial hands in the face of a deteriorating social weal, is consideration of the appropriate role of private philanthropy. It is the feeling of this observer that only a system supported by the society as a whole[14] can provide a reliable safety net. Private philanthropy can supplement what government cannot afford or chooses not to provide, but it cannot replace it.

---

14 Which we call government!

In normal times, private philanthropy should serve as society's risk capital – to test, model, explore what is not yet proven or may be controversial. It must be allowed to do so in arts, education and other quality of life endeavors as well as in the human service sector.

In abnormal times such as these, it may well be argued that there are emergent human tragedies that need immediate attention. But even as private philanthropy may choose to step into the breach, its mandate must be to advocate for where long-term funding should come from: as normalcy returns, government must assume its proper role – to protect the legitimate needs and rights of its citizens. It is surely appropriate for private philanthropy to redress suffering and need; it is at least as crucial for the independent philanthropic sector to advocate public policy that will place the primary responsibility for this where it properly belongs.

28%, 35% Deduction –
Does it Really Matter?
- March 9th, 2009 -

Many in our field have filed their carefully worded demurral to one element of the proposed stimulus plan; that of capping the maximum tax perfectibility (for US taxpayers) for charitable deductions at 28%. Their argument is that it would discourage charitable giving - at exactly the moment that the country and the world needs to encourage as much generosity as possible. As sympathetic as I am to the real value to our society of encouraging charitable giving and personal generosity, I don't find myself aligned with what seems to be the consensus in the philanthropy world. At the risk of antagonizing my potential clients and jeopardizing referrals (in these times, even we need to think about that!), I would like to suggest that it is a short-term problem but not an appropriate matter on which to do battle.

My thinking:

1. Any deductibility based on percentage of total gift is, to some degree arbitrary. Do we have any long-term evidence that a 35% deduction really does stimulate more charitable giving than 28%? If so, why not argue for 50%? Or, if one really believes that we are relieving government of its burden, why not a dollar-for-dollar deduction?

2. Most of the studies I have seen over the past several years show that tax benefit is NOT the top reason for philanthropic giving.

Those inclined to give, do so. Those not inclined to give, don't - even with tax incentives. What does seem to be true is that the structures of how one gives are tax motivated, but not whether to give. (There are many countries where there are very limited tax benefits from charitable giving, yet large segments of the societies choose to participate in the voluntary sector. If that is the case, then shouldn't the energies be more directed toward encouraging voluntarism rather than a detail of the tax code?

3. It is entirely possible that, in the very short run, there will be some impact in reducing the maximum percentage. And given these times, it would be cavalier indeed to dismiss any potential reduction in charitable giving. But I don't believe that this would be a long-term impact. My instinct is that charitable giving would revert to a previous level as incomes start improving. And therefore...

4. Let's not lose sight of the much, much larger impact, psychologically and financially of the current financial meltdown. The impact of having only 50% of one's net worth is far more influential in charitable choice than the tax code. And, as I have heard (and written about some months ago), many families are concerned about whether there will be enough for themselves or their heirs looking ahead. How much to leave for philanthropic purposes is far more motivated by a perception of, "Will there be enough," than, "How much for Uncle Sam."

5. Finally, the big picture. Private philanthropy is a huge sector and an indispensable one to our society for many reasons about which I

have written extensively elsewhere. But most social and human needs cannot be solved through private philanthropy alone. These needs require long-term social policy commitment. In other words, hunger is solved more by government food stamps than private soup kitchens. Job fairs are useful at the micro level but when unemployment is at 8-10%, those job fairs don't alleviate the need for benefits for millions. Given the benefits afforded to the richest Americans over the past 8 years or so, perhaps it is a time for the most affluent and philanthropic among us to accept a forgone tax benefit for the greater good of a society in need of our largess of spirit as much as our largess of dollars.

Giving in a Time of Less

R ecently I have been contacted by several reporters asking about how the predicted recession is going to influence philanthropy. Will donors stop giving? What now?

Foundation leaders and independent funders are asking me, "What should I do now?"

This is the not the first time we have faced economically challenging times. Fortunately or not, we have learned some things from the past. Here is my advice to funders about how to navigate in a time of shrinking resources.

First, some general observations:

1. Philanthropy typically trails the economy by between one and two years.

Funders typically make their commitments prospectively. Thus, when their resources are growing, they promise to give more in the upcoming period. When resources are shrinking, they will commit to fewer and smaller donations.[15] Psychology plays a significant role in how a funder views his or her resources, so it often takes longer to turn giving to the upside, even after it is evident that an economic recovery is on the way.

2. Economic downturns force funders to focus.

When more money is available, it is easy to give more dollars, and to give to more causes. When there are

---

[15] See exceptions below.

fewer dollars to dispense, marginal commitments fall away and even long-term commitments may be reviewed for their consistency with the "mission" of the donor or foundation.

3. When the economy is down, funders receive more requests to support basic human services.

And, objectively, there is a lot more need for these services. Unemployment, at-risk families, homelessness, hunger, and health needs all increase during tough times and there are fewer governmental dollars available to meet them. Funders who typically focus on other causes are forced to consider whether meeting basic needs is now more important. We know that immediate crises and tragedies (e.g., Katrina) bring out significant compassion giving, but funders do not always respond to large-scale economic readjustment and dislocation.

4. Funders who usually give to or through umbrella or re-granting charities will find that these charities are responding to the human needs arising out of the economic downturn.

They can feel comfortable that their dollars are meeting these emergent needs. Funders who usually give on a project basis, or to particular recipient organizations, will be challenged to rethink their priorities.

Next, some recommendations for funders:

1. Refocus

Re-examine your giving. Take a look at whether or not your giving is aligned with your mission. Sometimes it takes a financial shake-up or possible cutbacks to focus the mind and your budget.

2. Exit Strategies

Think carefully about how cutting back your giving during an economic downturn will effect the organizations you care about. As a funder, you do not have a legal obligation to continue to fund an organization unless you have made a multi year or project related commitment. But in some circumstances, there is a moral/ethical responsibility to continue to fund an organization or a project.

If your gift is incidental or incremental to a recipient organization's budget, you can, in perfectly good conscience, discontinue funding immediately after any current commitments are paid off. Your $1000 annual gift to your alma mater is hardly going to jeopardize the existence of that university if discontinued. But if your contribution or grant represents long-term core support, and the organization depends on your support for its basic budget, you need to think about the effect that reducing your contribution may have.

Although no funder MUST fund any organization indefinitely, you should think about how to curtail your support. Consider a gradual phase out. And give the recipient organization early notice about your plan. Some long-term funders who choose to discontinue their annual core support contribute an exit lump sum toward an endowment. In any case, responsible funders are aware of the impact of their giving on recipient organizations, and takes the time to think through their role in that relationship.[16]

3. Compassion Funding

Some funders believe that in times of economic challenge, when resources are shrinking, philanthropists

---

[16] Of course, it is my view that every gift should have an exit strategy in mind from the very beginning.

should rise to the occasion and maintain their level of giving from the good times. After all, they argue, now is the time when the non-profit sector needs support more than ever. Thus, some foundations argue that the 5% may be a fine base for normal years, but during hard times, they should maintain their previous giving level, even though they will far exceed the 5% minimum. And individuals, especially high net worth individuals, will often dig deeper to support causes and institutions to which they have devoted themselves, knowing that marginal giving from less devoted supporters will most assuredly diminish.

4. Advocacy Funding

My readers know that I believe strongly that funders should not shrink from funding advocacy. Charitable giving, driven by compassion, can never take the place of government support for people at risk. The size and complexity of our society is simply too great. But government spending is also influenced by economic downturns. If government income is down, the government will have to prioritize and decide how to allocate scarce resources. If we believe that the hungry should be guaranteed a meal, who should have the ultimate responsibility to provide the safety net? Whatever my personal view of the answer to this question, in tough times the funding community should be willing to support organizations that address the policies which provide for basic human needs.

5. Non-Financial Support for Non-Profit Sector

In a time of cutbacks organizations need all kinds of help. As contributions diminish, income from fees may fall, and volunteers may be too busy earning a living to help out in the office or in the tutoring program. As someone who cares about the cause, consider giving your time as well as your money to help the organizations you care about survive until the next bull market.

6. Keep Your Powder Dry

For many funders, the response to previous crises and disasters has led to a very different mandate at this time. For some, it was sobering to learn that the immediate massive funding didn't solve or anticipate the problems that arose one or two years later, long after all that compassion funding dissipated. Some funders have decided that in these cases it is not ideal to be a first responder, but rather to be able to respond to new and often unanticipated needs later on.

Some other funders have chosen to stay true to their primary mission. They argue that society will always need cultural or educational institutions or innovative organizations. If they are abandoned now, they will only be weaker later. If they were ignored now, they would only need to be rediscovered later. Better, they argue, to keep these institutions going and viable than to have to reinvent them when times are better.

7. A Concluding Thought

Both philanthropy and public policy are reflections of the values and vision of a society. America has a well-deserved reputation for its private generosity and philanthropic institutions. America also has a well-deserved reputation for public insensitivity to its most at-risk populations. Perhaps at no point in the past have these two tendencies been more in tension with one another. How we respond to the coming difficult times will tell us something about the American character in this decade.

Tsunami
The Philanthropic Responsibility
Beyond Today

- January 7th, 2005 -

Yesterday, I had occasion to hear a long time relief worker describe her experience in Sri Lanka and Indonesia this week. It reminded her of the immediate post-World War II reaction and behavior of Holocaust survivors. They spent months asking, searching, beseeching and pleading for any information about their families, friends, neighbors – their binding connections rent asunder by a human crime beyond comprehension. They had no homes, jobs, lives to which to return. It took years to provide the latter; the former were lost forever.

The widespread devastation of the Tsunami of 2004, a natural disaster, has called forth an unprecedented generosity from individuals throughout the world. Literally hundreds of millions of dollars has been pledged and paid from caring and concerned citizens of the world, including millions in the United States, whose deepest empathy was touched by the devastation visible on their TV screens.

By this time, I am sure that most of us connected with Stratus have participated in one way or another, generously and with care and compassion. Many have assumed leadership in their industries or communities. And by this time, all of us have been alerted to the potential for scams and to the most effective ways to verify the validity of the seekers. These comments, then, are directed for our thinking as we move beyond immediate relief to the long-term implications of our philanthropic response:

- Catastrophes are NOT the time for individual projects or high-risk venture philanthropy. It *is* a time for proven direct service organizations, such as the Red Cross, or Oxfam, or CARE, or Doctors without Borders (to name but a few), which have on the scene infrastructures, to do what they do best.

- Gifts to special relief efforts sponsored by our churches or synagogues or fraternal organizations, etc. are not wasted, but only when they too direct their gifts to established and proven international relief organizations.

- Disasters have both immediate and long-term needs. Feeding and clothing those who have nothing provide for the short-term; rebuilding cities and businesses and providing counseling for orphans and grieving parents is long-term. Those of us involved in philanthropic efforts have learned from 9/11 and other tragedies that we must not lose interest after the pictures disappear from the morning and evening news.

- In keeping with these needs, it is NOT unethical or immoral or irresponsible for relief agencies to hold something back for the longer term.

- Justified concern for the immediate should not blind us to persistent and pandemic human needs which transcend this moment, these places, and this part of the world. The number of children who die each year from malnutrition makes the number of deaths from the tsunami seem but a drop in the bucket; the number who are now dying from AIDS in parts of the world far exceeds these numbers, and with little relief in sight. Illiteracy, disease, and dislocation are often disasters with human causes and human solutions. We must not avert our eyes to those causes around the world or at home even as we respond appropriately and philanthropically to the calamity before us.

Those of us who are connected with *Stratus* are among the world's most blessed. It is incumbent upon us to demonstrate our capacity for giving, and our vision for rebuilding a world too easily broken – by acts of nature and of mankind.

Sign of the Times?

- June 6ᵗʰ, 2008 -

S peaking professionally (i.e. getting paid) is an important part of my professional identity and my annual income and has been for a long time. Eleven years ago, when I was still living in DC, in an effort to improve my skills, I applied to be a mentee in a program sponsored by the Washington Chapter of the National Speakers Association.

For me, the program more than did its job. I believe that it helped me polish some presentation skills and discipline by over 50% in 6 months. I went from being a person who spoke a lot to being an effective and sometimes even eloquent public speaker (and certainly more in demand).

Shortly thereafter, I moved to New York City, became a professional member of *The National Speakers Association* and joined the local chapter. I was so appreciative of what I had learned that I offered to help develop a mentoring program in the NY area. However, for reasons that were never clear to me, there was never an interest in doing so. So the idea sat dormant for several years until the current leadership expressed openness to the idea.[17]

There was enthusiastic response to the invitation to apply to become a mentee – many more completed applications or inquiries than would be possible to accommodate. And most of the applicants had excellent

---

[17] So much so that it was publicly announced before any of the details were even in place; and since those details are not of great significance to this piece, I will skip ahead....

and persuasive reasons why they would be appropriate mentees.

What did surprise me, though, was the paucity of interest in becoming a mentor. This surprised me because in every other mentoring situation I have ever been connected to, it has been considered a prestigious and highly desired thing to be asked to become a mentor. It means that one's skills, accomplishments, professional empathy are all being recognized. In one example, it was so competitive that mentees got to choose among 3 possible mentors! Not to be selected was a true "downer."

The leaders of the local NSA were similarly surprised and did some asking around – and what they learned was sobering indeed. For many, the economy is taking a toll. Mentoring requires a commitment of time to be sure, but that didn't seem to be the issue. What seemed more telling was the concern about polishing the skills of a possible competitor. Altruism and professional sharing was disposable faced with a potential cutback in income.

It is hard for me to know how accurate those perceptions are – but they tell me a lot about the current ethos. One might think that it is in times of stress and challenge that we dig deeper into our most charitable selves, and help those colleagues and friends and neighbors in need of our support. Surely there seems to be plenty of evidence that people are willing to go to the Gulf States to volunteer or bemoan Darfur and Myanmar. But is it possible that the closer things are to home, the more proximate the risk, the tighter our literal and figurative wallets become?

How Much – and For Whom?
- September 29, 2008 -

A ll of us on the philanthropy advising side of things are used to having private conversations with families about succession. While most of that has to do with when and whom to involve in decision making for family giving, it is not uncommon for this to lead to a conversation about other related matters. One related matter is how much to leave children and grandchildren, how much is too much, and when should they get it. These are always sensitive discussions and by the time the question is raised with me, it has typically been a quiet source of concern for some time.

The current economic debacle has recast the discussion: in the past, the issue has been raised in the quiet of a closed door office or living room, rarely raised as a public matter. Usually, such questions emerge from trying to balance a desire to encourage a healthy ethic among second and third generation families while allowing some of the benefits of inherited wealth. And it often reflects the dynamic tension of wanting to do well for society and right by one's offspring. Moreover, in private, one can articulate to an objective advisor the concerns about differing values and capabilities of one's children and grandchildren and how to be fair and equitable in dealing with those differences.

But twice, in two separate communities in recent weeks, in presentations before gatherings of families of means, all with a tradition of charitable giving, the question was raised publicly. The question didn't catch me off guard but the public nature did. Surely these folks didn't intend to share their ambivalences about their wayward or prideful or greedy or do-good kids in these settings; something else must be going on.

The issue, it seems, has taken on new meaning in the face of an insecure economy. If one's net worth can drop precipitously overnight, how much is enough to guarantee anything to one's children? If family health care or education for your grandchildren or subsidies for family gatherings are important, can you chance leaving your money to charitable causes? Or conversely, if you feel that some of your money must go to make some part of the world a better place, shouldn't you guarantee that commitment, even at the risk of imposing on your grandchildren to make it on their own? And if there is money available now to make a difference, given economic uncertainly, should one wait until some later point to do so? Or is responsible stewardship of a family legacy to reduce external spending to charities, no matter how worthy the cause, to guarantee the security of your flesh and blood?

These are not new questions, but what seems to be emerging is a shifting balance that uncertainty brings about. The question seems now to be driven not by HOW MUCH is enough, but rather to be motivated by IF there will be enough, and for whom. The discussions are just beginning, but I suspect that the much-ballyhooed transfer of wealth theories, which have informed the philanthropic thinking of many, are in for a serious challenge. Buckle up.

Readers may be surprised how many words are directed to this question. Yet in my experience it is one of the most continuing questions on the minds of funders. I have learned that it speaks to the deepest aspirations for philanthropy – what should one's legacy be? How does or should one involve future generations of a family? Should one trust any institutions with permanent endowments? Is it even good for the institutions to do that?

Fortunately past and current generations have given us lots of articulate spokespeople for all the points of view. It is always useful to remember what Julius

Rosenwald and Andrew Carnegie thought. The issue has arisen very publicly with Bill Gates, Warren Buffet, and Michael Bloomberg making it clear that they don't believe in perpetuity.[18]

It is also striking to see how the question of perpetuity is now being asked in new ways by a younger generation of philanthropists. Their thinking has certainly made me reexamine my own.

---

[18] Is it possible that they are all confident enough in the immortality of their own names that they don't feel they need to do so through their philanthropy? Just a thought.

Section Two:

Philanthropy in Our Lives:
How to Do It "Wisely"

Chapter Four:

Perennial Questions

T he world has been very good to you. And you, your accountant, and your money manager all agree that it is both cost effective, tax advantageous, and right, to give back. The only problem is how to decide and how to do it wisely. Beginning with this month's column, we will explore a variety of strategies for giving, each reflecting a different approach, and each suggesting one effective way of deciding how to express *your* philanthropic style.

No one has enough to give to everything. All of us say "no" every time we throw away an unwanted mail solicitation or hang up on an intrusive phone call. And the more successful we become, the more people perceive us as walking dollar signs, leading to even more unwanted and intrusive solicitations.

It is never easy to say "no" graciously; but it is even harder to say "yes" wisely. Yet as long as you are going to be giving, you want to make a difference, accomplish good for the world – and feel good about doing it. Friends, colleagues, business associates, your alma mater, and any other place where you may have trod all have very good ideas how you can spend your philanthropic dollars.

In this space, we will be exploring collaborations, partnerships, venture philanthropy, family involvement, long-term and short-term commitments, investment policies, and other emerging philanthropic approaches – all with an eye to helping you determine the best way for you to decide, and for your generosity and philanthropy to accomplish all that you want it to be. Stay tuned.

A Walking Dollar Sign

- September 2004 -

"**I** need you to protect me from myself," one client told me. "Whenever I walk into a room, I am solicited – and I have trouble saying "no." Afterwards, I often feel taken advantage of."

It reminded me of the day, some years ago, when my appointment as head of the Bronfman Foundation was announced. My wife and I happened to be at a reception in Washington. At the end of the evening, she said, "we must be careful to avoid becoming cynical – all evening, people kept asking me to help them get funding." And I hadn't even begun!

Those of us who are funders or are known to be of means often find ourselves to be walking dollar signs. It is amazing how good looking, clever, wise, insightful, and popular we are, as long as there is still a possibility of funding. It is easy to become cynical.

But, while we must be cautious of those who flatter and fawn, we mustn't become cynical. There are real needs and valid causes. There are untested innovative solutions, and established but under funded agencies. Our resources, wisely given and thoughtfully administered, can and do make a difference. Some will choose an advisor or intermediary to filter, protect, and evaluate; others will enjoy the direct engagement with potential recipients. Philanthropy, done well, gives gratification to the donor, and does well by the recipient.

Walking under the dollar sign needn't be a hindrance; it is a noble challenge to think strategically about our philanthropy, and a blessing to be able to do well, to do good, and to help improve our world.

Non-Profit Pay –
Who Should Be Subsidizing Whom?
- *March 2008* -

I was flattered to read an issue of *CON-TRIBUTE* magazine from December 2007, and discover that I was quoted, and even had my picture connected to an article about the Pay Gap in the non-profit/independent sector.

I am comfortable with the quote attributed to me but I do believe that the article as a whole focuses on the wrong part of the equation. The issue seems to take issue with the large wage gap between the highest paid executives in the sector vs. the lowest wage earners. And while the article most assuredly takes note of staff burnout, retention, and wage disparity with the for-profit sector, one might read the article to imply that the greatest challenge to credibility of the sector is the compensation for those at the top.

It may or may not be true that some in this sector are overpaid but frankly it is the wrong question. The most important question, which should be high on the agendas of all donors and funders, is NOT whether there should be limits on excess pay. The real question is the unconscionable low pay and absence
of fringe benefits afforded to so many in this sector. Congress and well-meaning hand wringers may feel that no one in this sector should be receiving a compensation package that competes with the private sector at the upper level. But shouldn't the in-

dignation be that non-profit organizations are allowed and sometimes encouraged to pay people poverty or below-market level wages and not offer fringe benefits!! I wish that our charity rating services penalized such organizations, and that independent funders and government grants mandated appropriate level salaries and benefits.

If funders made it clear that such low salaries are in fact abusive, and were willing to fund appropriately, it would make a much stronger statement about the credibility of and respect due to these fields of service than all the articulated concerns about filling the anticipated leadership gap.

The Perpetuity Question

- November 16th, 2007 -

Any casual observer of the philanthropy field has noted the crescendo of debate about the legitimacy and/or wisdom of perpetuity of endowments and foundations. The classic debate isn't new: does one protect ones commitments and values by setting up a permanent fund which, in theory, engages future generations and supports one's areas of concern for as long as one can imagine OR does one support one's interests now on the basis that a dollar spent today is worth and accomplishes more than five cents on the dollar every year?

The debate has become more vocal with the addition of several other considerations: do endowments keep nonprofits from being agile and responsive to changing conditions *or* do they protect the investment in facilities and cushion against the inevitable fads in philanthropy?

When heavyweights like the Gates' and Buffets weigh in on spend-down, it makes everyone sit up and take notice and that has led to a trend (hard to quantify!) to lean toward spend-down of philanthropic trusts and foundations. The question must be asked: are we better off with each generation taking responsibility for its own societal needs or are we better off with capital which has been preserved and reserved for that purpose?

On an individual basis, of course, it isn't a "societal" value but a personal one. I remember one friend (not a client), a well-known philanthropist, who sought my advice on whether to adopt a perpetuity or spend-down approach. This family foundation is known for its extraordinary commitment to young people, so I anticipated that the answer would be obvious. Of course they would want to maintain the involvement of future generations. But I was wrong; the longer we talked the more clear it became that the policy would be to spend it down in the lifetime of the founders, and not be left for the future. Their perception was that it would be both a burden and challenge for them to honor the "donor intent."

To take an opposite example, in another case, the donor left responsibility for a foundation in his estate without instructions except that it last in perpetuity. The heirs didn't even know that the foundation existed!

To complicate matters, US law allows but does not guarantee perpetuity. With a 5% payout mandate for private foundations, a series of down years can erode the principle sufficiently that, even with the intention of permanence, it cannot be guaranteed.[19]

But these personal issues and values don't answer the larger societal one about whether such permanence is a good or bad thing. For the sake of staking out a position to challenge our readers, I

---

[19] The law does not call for a floating payout rate, linked to some moving target such as earnings, cost of living, etc., even though that would probably be wiser and more equitable; in up years, more money for public good would be mandated, but in down years, a lesser amount payout would be required.

have come to the conclusion that perpetuity is a good thing:

1. It guarantees that there is an independent source of risk capital to address emerging challenges to civil society that may neither be popular nor funded by tax dollars.

2. When properly thought through, it allows a set of values to inform future generations, a legacy of values that may transcend a legacy of money or name.

3. When properly defined, it guarantees that capital gifts are not wasted by providing for deferred maintenance and long-term attention that would otherwise compete with operating dollars.

4. When ethically managed and governed, it guarantees that there is a cohort of citizens who are forced to think responsively and responsibly about unanticipated needs with autonomy not possible by those in the public sector.

5. If those who have made significant sums are worried about the deleterious effect of inherited wealth, a permanent foundation can allow a productive transfer of responsibility without the questionable productivity of unearned wealth.

Taking Risks

Most of the essays in this book were written before the current financial meltdown and for a variety of settings and audiences. Yet the issue of risk tolerance is one of the most tender spots in funder sensitivities. I am quite sensitive to those who are risk averse in their investment strategies and in their funding approaches. Stewardship is not to be taken lightly. And given the investment adventures of too many foundations, one can hardly criticize those who stayed true to conservative (with a small "c" to be sure) principles even in times of creative returns.

Yet there are too many funders who are risk averse when they think they are supporting innovation, change, or simply new projects. Too often their words and funding strategies don't align – or they haven't fully confronted their own tolerance for failure. A failed project, which has been funded thoughtfully, is not a failed strategy. In fact, in many cases it may reflect the very best funding strategy. These essays invite funders to think carefully about where they truly fit, and, when appropriate, take a deep breath and allow for the possibility that some of the best ideas are high risk, and definitely worth it.

"Making a Difference"

- May 17th, 2004 -

T here it was again. Another foundation with "making a difference" in their mission statement. This time, it was a community foundation at whose annual meeting I was asked to speak.

The annual report boasted of the many established organizations that received grants from their unrestricted pool; it proudly celebrated the manifold local, national and international agencies that were beneficiaries of donor advised or restricted funds; and they enticed potential donors to endow their annual gifts to their favorite charities through an endowment invested with them. All true, good, worthy, and responsible.

But, "making a difference?" Difference means that something is changed because of one's involvement, beneficence, generosity, or foresight. Where, I wondered, were the investments in the young idealists whose ideas need seed money to test out? I looked in vain for the capital for innovative local programming in the arts, culture, education, or health care? In a city where venture capital is the means by which many of the wealthy gain their prominence, where was the venture capital for the next great idea or project?

Making a difference means taking a risk. To fund the same old university, hospital, symphony, church or synagogue, or museum is legitimate and deserving. Don't stop! But philanthropists who spend their time looking for the next high flier in business might do well to set aside a portion of their philanthropic dollars for higher risk ventures in the not-for-profit realm. Indeed, any new venture, any untested idea, any unproven young professional, any budding artist may fail, or fall short, or disappoint, or disappear. But without such risks, our social weal will be much the same as it was before your involvement. And, if it is the same as it was without your support, is that really making a difference?

Risk & Risk Aversion
in Philanthropic Foundations

- February 10th, 2005 -

We have just finished the big charitable contribution season. Donors and foundations have made their annual distributions. Our civic responsibility has been done and the stack of envelopes on our desks has finally diminished. But many of us are left with the big question: Are my gifts making a difference?

What do we mean when we talk about "making a difference?" Making a difference means causing change. Something in this world will change because of funding. But how committed are we really to change? In my experience as CEO of a large international foundation and an advisor to individual funders, there is a huge chasm between what we say we want and our willingness to fund it.

There are some understandable reasons for our failure of nerve. Funding change involves risk, and risk entails the possibility of failure. And who takes pride in failure? Imagine that you are the chairperson of a foundation reporting to your board. Would you like to report that a substantial percentage of the grants that you have made have been unsuccessful? Would you be willing to recommend that your foundation emphasize funding high-risk ventures at the expense of investing in likely successes?

There is, of course, nothing wrong with funding "safe" causes. There are many serious problems that can best be addressed with conventional methods. Large and well-established institutions may be in the best position to implement tried and true solutions. Donors to such institutions can be confident that their dollars will be spent responsibly. They can take pride in their gifts and garner the prestige that comes with them. The not-for-profit world relies on this kind of giving.

But this kind of giving does not "make a difference." Making change requires a different kind of donor. The donor that is willing to think out of the box, to fund start-ups with new and untested ideas, to challenge the common wisdom. A donor, in other words, with risk tolerance.

Very few donors have a high degree of risk tolerance. Sometimes donors can be enticed to join a partnership and collaboration. They will fund an experiment if they can share the risk. But even when they do, they often do not have the patience to see a risky start-up venture through its early, shaky years to see the outcome.

What I have described here is the well-known, essentially conservative nature of grantmaking. It is not surprising, but for many years I nonetheless found it puzzling. After all, many donors have acquired their wealth precisely by taking risks in business. Why suddenly, when they become philanthropists, do they play it safe?

I found an answer in the classroom. In my courses at NYU on the subject of philanthropy, I ask my students – all donors and grantmakers themselves – to simulate an allocation process. I present them with a docket of potential grantees – including both "safe" and "risky" alternatives.

First, each student decides, on his or her own, a preliminary allocation. At this stage there is always a great deal of variation among the students' selections. Many do select the "risky" grantees.

Yet in the second stage, when the students must come to a group decision about the allocation of funds among the potential grantees, the result is totally different. Invariably, the group will allocate funds only to the safest of grantees. The student who began the process excited by innovative ideas defers to another who shudders at the chance for failure. And as each student argues for a different grantee, the group as a whole becomes persuaded that the only responsible way to express their stewardship is to select the least controversial, and the least risky proposals. The group process leads inexorably to risk aversion.

Watching how my students make decisions in the classroom has taught me a valuable lesson. No, not that boards and allocations processes are inherently unwieldy and subject to all too predictable conservatism, as true as this lesson is. Rather, a funder or funding organization must confront its own bottom line – if the stated mission is to be a "change agent", "to make a difference", to impact a field of service, then that organization would do well to put the issue of risk and risk aversion on the table prior to the allocation process. It is more likely to understand its own predilection or organizational culture, and much more likely to make some room for those innovative and cutting edge experiments which may indeed make all the difference.

Chapter Five:

How-To

The original intent for this book was to be a collection of opinion pieces, not a "how-to" manual. My thinking was that there are already so many quite good books and articles. Why not simply refer folks to that which is already well worn?

I was dissuaded from that by students and clients alike. They urged me to include some of the reality and richness that has emerged from my practice to provide real hands-on examples for readers. So what, they argued, if others have written about the same things. They enjoyed learning from me; why shouldn't others?

I was convinced that they are right based on my speaking experience. Early in my career, when I was more truly an academic, I had great ideas and was probably a much better intellectual thinker than I am today. But I was not as good a storyteller. I learned, somewhat late in my career, that there is no inherent conflict between thoughtfulness and interesting. It matters that the ideas are coherent and engaging.

What follows in this chapter and the next are "practica." While not a comprehensive manual, the chapters do address, in real and useful ways, the kinds of choices and decisions many funders have to make. And all, as you will see, are based on real life experiences of others who had to ask the same questions and think about their decisions.

Chapter 5-A:

Philanthropy Advising

Philanthropy Advising – What is That?

A dmittedly, it isn't a typical profession. People who want money assume it is a direct line to a charitable ATM. People who have it often wonder how much of their money we want. Even within the field, it can mean different things. For some, it deals exclusively with money management, about trusts, or donor advised funds or investment strategies. For others, it is about management of philanthropic giving for a family, foundation, or funder. For wealth managers and trust and estate attorneys, it is often relegated to the "soft" area, not fully worthy of their time or as measureable as their results. So, I have often found myself explaining what I do to an incredulous or puzzled listener. And perhaps to help that understanding along, I am including a couple of pieces that address the question: what is that?

Philanthropic Advisor

What Does That Mean?

- May 2ⁿᵈ, 2008 -

I t shouldn't bother me, I guess, but it does. And it happened again just this week. Someone again asked me how the fund-raising is going. When I explained that I don't have anything to do with fundraising but only work on the side of funders (advising, teaching, speaking…) they expressed their surprise. They remembered that I did philanthropic advising but they somehow assumed that meant fundraising.

Now the obvious observation is that I probably don't have a very good "elevator speech". After all, I spend my professional time helping people develop strategies to *give* money, not *raise* it. Should that be so hard to explain? It seems that I, for one, haven't found a good way to say it so people get it – at least in a way that they remember.

But, you ask, so what? Is it really a problem? Isn't it just the other side of the table? And why do I care so much?

To be fair, there are those colleagues who don't make the distinction that I do. They feel that helping to raise money is in fact helping people give thoughtfully, and advising those who give is in fact helping to support worthy institutions and genuine needs. As long as they are clear what role they are playing, they don't feel any professional conflict of interest in doing both.

I do. While I deeply respect those who feel comfortable advising on both sides, I find that it doesn't work for me. For, as I see it, advising those who want to think about giving requires that I be fully independent in my advising. If I am to give an opinion or judgment, there should be no possibility that I have a perceived conflict of interest. If I am to work with those of varying generations within the same family, none of them should feel that I favor one approach because of competing commitments. If I were to advise a philanthropist or foundation on their funding focus, they would be suspicious if they heard that a potential grantee was paying me to help raise funds.

It is not simply being on the other side of the table. Giving wisely requires being informed by an entirely different set of concerns, ethics, priorities, judgments, policies, and processes than fundraisers.[20]

For me, helping people and funding organizations to make wise funding decisions, appropriate for their needs and style and priorities, is a profession and an art form of its own and calls for different knowledge and skill sets than fundraising. I like to think that my insistence on the difference is because I have learned that difference, and not simply because I haven't yet developed a good elevator speech.

---

[20] In a workshop I do both at an NYU class and independently, where people roleplay both sides, they are almost always shocked to discover how different the questions and starting points are from one another.

The Hard "Soft" Questions

A recent study, as reported by *Private Wealth*, revealed a surprising level of dissatisfaction with the work of Trust and Estate attorneys. The suggestive statistic, which led to the study, was the surprisingly high percentage of high net-worth families and individuals who never signed off on their proposed estate plans.

I suspect that many of these lawyers have long-term relationship with their clients and deal with many other legal matters on a regular basis. It wouldn't surprise me at all to hear the lawyers retort that even if their clients may not have signed off on a full comprehensive estate plan, they have approved many of the components as independent pieces.

I am not an attorney or an expert in general estate planning, so I am reluctant to comment on all of the issues suggested by the study. For me, the most telling comment had to do with payment and follow up. Since, as reported by the study, attorneys have little incentive to follow up with their clients as they are paid for the work they do, not for its success. Moreover, in a matter not discussed in the article, in many cases, the attorneys are often named trustees of the estates and foundations and would argue that they are well aware of the intent of their clients in implementing their thinking. Unstated is that they will be paid for this post-mortem work as well, a sensitive issue on which I will comment below.

The study revealed that many otherwise intelligent and successful high net-worth individuals have found these proposals so complex and incomprehensible that they simply didn't feel comfortable signing off on them. That may be true. My experience is restricted to the area of philanthropy, and my observations are exclusively from that perspective. What I have seen in many cases is that very caring lawyers have set up the structures of a philanthropic plan, but have not thought it through. There was no question of its legality, but there was a lot of question about its functionality as a useful device for the family to implement – or even understand – the philanthropic values and expectations of the trust or foundation, or of the one who authorized its creation.

Part of this has to do with an interesting dilemma for lawyers: unless otherwise specified, a lawyer must respond to his/her client, in almost all cases the individual who is setting up the estate. For people like me who advise exclusively on philanthropy matters, the "client" is typically the whole family. A philanthropy plan should anticipate matters of succession and inclusion and not simply immediate governance; it needs an understanding of legacy and not simply legitimacy; it needs to clarify parameters of giving without straight-jacketing future decision makers; it should inform on questions of perpetuity or time limits; it should convey values and not simply worth.

Of course, these are not the issues most lawyers are trained to deal with. The challenges I often find in family foundations, responsibility for which arises after the death of the founder, are that the attorney simply did not know "philanthropy." In some cases, as mentioned above, there is self-interest on the part of the attorney. By managing the trust and being the managing trustee of the foundation, there would be a continuing fee – and I know of numerous second and third generation family members who have resented that pre-condition. However, I don't want to paint too broad a charge; to give the benefit of the doubt, I believe that in most cases, the lawyer believes that he or she has at heart the best interests of the family and his/her erstwhile client in this arrangement. The shortcomings are not because of intent; they are because of the absence of early involvement of someone with philanthropy expertise.

Incidentally, while the article that stimulated this opinion piece speaks exclusively about T & E attorneys, one can easily make a very similar case about those who manage money. They may know a great deal about making money, of maximizing value, but philanthropy is about spending it, maximizing values, a different matter altogether.

You, as a reader, fully understand that I am a philanthropy advisor and educator so you can legitimately say that I have as much self-interest in this matter as the lawyer or wealth manager does. It is true that providing such advice is what "pays the rent." It is also true that I have done workshops for both wealth managers and lawyers on how to understand the philanthropy questions in working with their clients. But there are many more families and attorneys, many more money managers than will ever find or use me or any of my colleagues. The vast majority of their clients don't need our expertise. Moreover, no one starts with a philanthropy advisor – even when we are consulted, we are at the end of the planning chain, long after the relationships with the attorney and wealth manager are established.

What would help most high net worth families and individuals is if their lawyers and money managers were to take the time to learn about how philanthropy works as a complement to their legal and investment training. Often they view that this "soft" information is not as important as the "hard" knowledge of law and investment strategy. My response: it is not accidental that the motto of our philanthropy advisory firm is "It is *hard* to say 'yes' wisely."

Chapter 5-B:

Teach Your Children Well

"Teach Your Children Well"

- May 31ˢᵗ, 2004 -

She is truly a wonderful philanthropist. She is one of the best venture philanthropists and a thoughtful donor. Her causes, always carefully considered, are local, national, and international in scope. She is involved and energetic – and respectful of the unique role of being one of the stewards in the third generation of a fortune developed by a well-known family enterprise. Her chosen career as a venture capitalist has helped expand the already ample means of this family.

Our discussion this time focused on how to teach philanthropy to her children. They are elementary school age, and she is proud that every week the family ritualistically sets aside money to give to charity. And she has a tradition of periodically discussing with her children why they are setting money aside and where it is going. What did I think?

If only everyone did that much, our world would be much the better, and we would be developing the next generation of philanthropists at an early age. I wondered aloud, could the kids really relate to the causes simply by putting money in a container? Gently, I proposed that for children that age, hands on involvement would mean at least as much. Feeding the hungry, building a house for homeless, visiting the sick teach that their money and their time are helping real people with real needs, and not very far from their own home.

There will be time enough for intellectualizing charity and philanthropy – but for the youngest, nothing teaches the meaning of caring more than demonstrating that you care.

Last month, we discussed how to introduce the younger budding philanthropists to the meaning of charitable giving – of oneself and of ones means. What about those teenagers? How does one teach adolescents about the meaning of philanthropy?

The best approach with adolescents is to use their peers to best advantage. Their friends have more influence than you do – certainly in terms of style and how to spend that precious private time.

At that age, it is best to encourage the beginnings of independent and autonomous decision making. Ideally, your community has a youth philanthropy initiative (check with your local community foundation). These initiatives model the entire cycle of grantmaking, from developing a mission to developing an RFP to soliciting proposals to studying requests to allocating funds. Some communities encourage families to set up small, restricted funds, and even match them!

The process can be individualized, but it works better if groups of teens are in it together. An experienced grantmaking pro can guide the process, communal leaders are flattered and excited to tell their stories to these young funders. And the responsibility to actually make a decision to say "yes" or "no" is a valuable life lesson.

The process itself is one of the most effective ways to learn that giving money away is not so easy. But it can be rewarding and meaningful, and, when done thoughtfully, can make a difference.

Isn't that a lesson that all of us involved in philanthropy need to remember - whatever our age?

Anonymity vs. Public Recognition

- June 2nd, 2005 -

They were wonderful clients. The family agreed on virtually everything about their new foundation; when to spend the money, which organizations should benefit, who should decide, how long should the foundation last... Their lawyer was almost right when he said he didn't understand why they needed me.

The clinker came when we discussed how to make certain gifts. One second-generation member wanted everything to be given anonymously; another could not imagine big enough neon signs. This unarticulated disagreement almost disrupted the foundation.

When I told this story recently, an audience member told me that a similar dispute had led to a six-month disagreement with his wife. They had agreed on a major gift to a school. One agreed with the school that it should bear their name; the other did not want their name on any institution.

There are legitimate arguments on both sides: the "anonymity" advocates say: why self aggrandize? Why have future generations labeled as the "rich kids"? Why invite everyone to feel they can knock on your doors for similar large gifts?

The publicity proponents want to affirm a concept of philanthropic leadership. You believe in this cause and want others to follow. Everyone knows you are wealthy, you should show what leadership means. Shouldn't the family legacy include evidence of your altruism as well as your affluence?

There is no one right way. Each family and foundation must seek its own level, respond to its own culture, and give in a way that satisfies its own mission. As long as you know why you choose one or the other, each can be a valid and noble way to give.

Art – The Unrequited Love

- August 10th, 2004 -

T heir home was featured that month on the cover of the home city magazine. Their resources were more than ample, sufficient that the community foundation on whose behalf I was speaking in that city, considered them one of their top families. Yet what concerned them at our meeting was their art collection.

Should they divide it among their friends and relatives? Should their will specify that it be sold and the proceeds divided? Should they give it as a collection to a museum with which they are connected?

The discussion was surprisingly emotion-laden. Most of their options were viable – but only after discussing them all was it clear that only one fit their needs. It became increasingly clear to me, and ultimately to them, that their passion for their art was unlike their other possessions and assets. The only decision that seemed right was that they should give their collection in its entirety to the local museum on whose board they sit.

I have seen this dynamic with numerous clients: what to do for relatives and charities and causes with their financial and real estate assets was easy. It was what to do with their art collections that they found almost impossible to solve. Perhaps it is because art becomes their signature, or their inanimate family, or because each piece is an unwritten story of life's journey.

Or, more than any other investment, the sole purpose of their art is to give pleasure. For many, the opportunity to extend that to others is the greatest legacy of all.

Should You Go It Alone?

- January 9th, 2009 -

Not everyone likes to go it alone. Philanthropy takes time, energy, trust, and risk. These are great attributes for generating wealth; they are also great attributes when you want to give it way.

Not everyone has the time or trusts his or her own instincts when it comes to charitable giving – rightly so. You know what it took to learn to make money well; you aren't sure you are ready to devote that to the giving side.

Some, of course, hire or contract with an advisor to help. Some give "safely" to worthy but unchallenging causes like their alma mater *United Way*, and to requests from friends. There are those, though who like the idea of doing it together with others – both to leverage their own philanthropic dollars, and to have the benefit of others knowledge and wisdom.

One of the most intriguing and newly popular ways to do that is through a funding collaborative. Typically, a small group chooses to pool a defined amount of money and make joint decisions about how, where, and when to spend it. These collaboratives might be comprised of friends, professional colleagues, or those who share a commitment to a particular cause. They can be initiated by a community foundation, an individual who has a passion, or a social group that decides to do something beneficial as well as fun. And they can function as a committee of the whole, have functioning subcommittees, or contract with a professional to provide staff support to the group.

Funding collaboratives are now found throughout the country. They include all age and demographic groups, but are often the way into philanthropy for women, younger funders, or those new to philanthropy. For a growing number of philanthropists, it is worth a look.

Since this question arises so frequently, I have developed a simple checklist that funders can use to determine if they or a project are appropriate to collaborating. While it is not an essay, I have included this worksheet for those who are enticed by or considering this mode of funding. Many clients have told me that they find it a useful planning guide.

Definitions:

> - Collaboration: a joint/coordinated effort by more than one funder to support an existing organization.
> - Partnership [Horizontal]: a joint/coordinated effort to organize, develop, run a project or program.
> - Vertical Partnership: a restricted or exclusive relationship between a cause or organization and a funder.

Why Partnerships and Collaborations?

> - To leverage funds.
> - To leverage influence.
> - To "save" money.
> - To enhance expertise.
> - To spread risk.

Projects that lend themselves best to Collaborations and Partnerships:

> - A clearly identified service deliverer which/who is respected by funders.
> - A discreet project/program (either based on time or content).
> - An innovative or BIG idea that benefits from mutual support.
> - A project that would have political or ideological limitations if it were done by existing group or through pre-existing relationships.

Not every grant should be a partnership... Conditions for effective partnerships:

> - Clarity and agreement on goals and scope of project.

> ➤ Willingness to surrender autonomy regarding decisions making, allocation procedures, and relationship with grantees.
> ➤ Clarity and agreement on governance and decision making.
> ➤ Clarity on length of agreement/project.
> ➤ Clarity on role of new participants/partners.
> ➤ Clarity on role, if any, of junior partners.
> ➤ Understanding that funder is both "owner" and funder at the same time.

Not every funder is suited to be a good partner. Who should NOT be a Partner funder?

> ➤ If you insist on your own independent allocation process...
> ➤ If you insist on renewing participation at an interval different than that of other funders...
> ➤ If you demand exclusive reporting system at odds with other funders...
> ➤ If you have an "involvement" culture or policy which is not consistent with other funders...
> ➤ If you have expectations or underlying goals which are not in keeping with others...

Finally, before you decide...

> ➤ Will all partners be equal or will there be a "managing" partner?
> ➤ Will all partners be putting the same amount into the project or will there be differential dollar commitments?
> ➤ Do all partners agree on an "exit strategy" or the potential for renewal of funding?
> ➤ Who will comprise the board? Or represent you in decision-making?
> ➤ What changes will the organization or project need to adopt to effectively deliver the desired outcomes?

> ➤ Have you considered what would happen if the project "fails"?
> ➤ Are you prepared to give the extra time and attention to your partners?

Partnerships and Mergers
The Hype and the Promise
- June 18th, 2009 -

The previous piece was written some time ago for the purpose of giving organizations a useful tool for the ifs and hows of partnerships and mergers. It is one of the most requested pieces I have ever written. It was based on fairly extensive experience in the area: both as the CEO of a foundation which invested heavily in such partnerships and as a periodic consultant to organizations which were exploring mergers and partnerships.

Any observer of the independent sector is well aware that this topic continues to be at the top of the agenda of many organizations and funders. The reasons are obvious and persuasive: are there duplications of services or back-office support that can be eliminated for immediate financial savings? Can one larger better-funded organization reach the scale to truly have an impact? Can a merged organization inspire influential volunteers/board members who might be less interested in smaller or more local initiatives? Is there a leveraging of influence which might impact public policy or encourage greater voluntary support if funders joined forces?

Over the last two or three years, the answers for many non-profits and for many funders to these questions has been "yes." Barely a week goes by without the announcement of another merger or partnership. It is time to take a glance to see if we are going the right direction.

Observation 1: *Takeover or merger?*

Upon close examination, most of the mergers are not true mergers except in name. In the vast majority of cases they are really take-overs by a stronger organization which identified a common interest or missing competence. The new organization may have a revised name and board, but it is rarely a merger of equals.

This probably represents one of the more successful models of organizational marriage. Success means that there are efficiencies and scale. Often there is a loser as well. The absorbed organization may find that its staff is soon considered expendable, its signature programs revised or replaced, and constituencies or locations once served by the absorbed organization don't make it past the new strategic plan.

This is not to say that there never is a value in such a takeover. The weaker organization may be truly vulnerable or fragile and may well have had to close; their prize programs may have outlived their value; funders may simply have lost interest in the unique constituencies. Such a takeover may serve to preserve and add value to programs and projects that would have been lost without them.

What makes these successful is when there is clarity ahead of time about what is really at stake, what the trade-offs will be, and who really will be in control. If there isn't a good self-awareness by both sides, resentment and resistance is likely to surface pretty quickly.

Observation 2: *Cultural compatibility*

The greatest challenge to successful partnerships and mergers is cultural incompatibility. While a shared mission, agreed funding, negotiated governance and staffing are necessary preconditions, they are insufficient. What is harder to determine but ultimately the most crucial component is if the 2 or more organizations have compatible cultures. These cultures don't have to be identical – they have to be compatible.

Most organizations would do well to avoid shotgun weddings and most funders would be wise to not force them. They would be better to try some joint projects, a shared planning effort, a mutual board retreat, a safe space for staff to converse openly with each other about their own organizations and visions for the future.

Some might argue that in these crisis times this kind of planning takes time, money, and risks the benefits of the merger. And they are correct that there is an investment which hard pressed organizations may feel they don't have. But these investments are not luxuries – they are essential. We have learned all too well that financial investments made with due diligence can be risky; investments made without them are downright dangerous. The same can be said with proposed mergers. Done too quickly or with too much naïveté can bring disaster and bring down two organizations quite quickly.

What is culture? The affective issues that say something about the style and character of any organizations. How are decisions made? How much empowerment or micromanagement is there? Do aesthetics matter? Is the workplace competitive or collegial? Is risk rewarded or penalized? And this is just the beginning.

Integration of programs may take time. Integration of cultures takes much longer.

The message for funders is that they/we need to be quite cautious in our trying to be directive and helpful to our grantees. What may seem obvious from a slight remove may be less so from the inside. The funder may be right, but only if the funder allows for the merger process to work its way carefully and thoughtfully.

Observation 3: *Efficiency ≠ Effectiveness*

Efficiency and scale may not always be the most effective way to achieve an end. As we saw in "observation 1", a merger may well lead to some external efficiencies. But if an entire constituency is abandoned because of it, is it always the most effective way to do things?

The pressure for scale and replicablity seems enticing. But only if the problem being solved is one that lends itself to scale and replicability. Food stamps work well because it is a large and easily applied solution; food pantries are much more dependent on local realities.

Funders much be careful to make sure that they are clear what problem they want to solve when they urge their grantees to scale up or to follow developed models. All too often programs and projects are viewed as cookie cutter solutions without adaption to local, regional, ethnic or cultural circumstances. Fortunately, among sophisticated funders this tendency has begun to ebb. But as the perception grows that good funding is to use leverage to encourage efficiency, there has been a surge among funders who haven't had the depth of experience to know how and when to use this leverage.

Observation 4: *Innovation matters*

Innovation matters. But innovation only occasionally comes from large bureaucratic organizations (and is particularly true during these times of stress when organizations are doing all they can to stay afloat). It is vital that there be as much commitment to continued innovation as there is to enhanced efficiency. Innovation and start-ups have a high failure rate, but the best innovation eventually becomes mainstream and predominant.

Let me be clear: I am not saying that funders should insist that they will only fund new projects even when it may be clear that the best grant is for operations or technical assistance. However, more than ever there are pockets of creativity that need start up or mezzanine funding. And while it may seem to be good practice to encourage these small free standing organizations to be adopted or absorbed or merged, funders who choose to encourage mergers and partnerships would do well to keep some of their funding dry to support start-ups on their own terms.

Certainly as every early investor knows, good exit strategy planning is key. There will be a time when the start up needs to sink, swim, swallow or be swallowed. Hopefully at the right time and not because of an externally motivated push for efficiency.

Observation 5: *Courage to Explore*

The first four observations might well be read as cautionary. I wouldn't want a reader to assume that these cautions suggest a resistance to partnerships and mergers. In fact, quite the contrary. It is probably true that never before has there been a better time. Survival challenges focus the mind. It is time for many organizations and projects to drop their isolation and self-importance. It is time for many organizations to look more closely at whether their business model is really sustainable looking forward. It is time for many organizations, which claim a transcendent mission, to confront whether they really believe it – and accept that fulfilling their mission may require surrendering their own autonomy. It is time for many organizations which have done many more things than they could possibly do well to drop the mediocre parts of their portfolios – for their own and for greater good. It is a time for courage, reinvention, and honest self-examination.

The caution is to do these things right – or at least as well as humanly possible. But avoidance is not the same as thoughtful and courageous exploration. It is time for nothing less.

Chapter Six:

The Marker Method

I don't believe that there is only one right or even best way to do something. And that is certainly true for those of us who advise funders and foundations to determine their own strategies. My contribution to the menu of options, the Marker Method, is not a suggestion that others don't do this work as well or effectively as I do. However, this approach has worked well in my work. It represents a somewhat different approach than the norm. I was urged to commit it to writing so that it can be more widely used or modified by my colleagues in the field, and to not just keep it as a proprietary approach.

As I suggest in more detail in the coming chapter, it is my experience that beginning with the "culture choices" rather than "value choices" turns out to be a more efficient way for groups to get to real decisions with a greater sense of the implications for others in the room. I begin with "culture" and end with "mission." Those who have used such techniques as Meyers Briggs or other "style" approaches will not be very surprised that this can be of assistance. It is presented here in published form for the first time. Perhaps you too will find it helpful to understand the dynamics in the room as you make funding decisions.

And if you do choose to use this method, let me know what worked, what didn't and what needs more amplification for future editions.

Step 1:
Understanding Your Funding Culture

- *Do you wish to support specific causes or institutions OR to keep the family together?*

Many family funders find themselves torn between a commitment to support specific causes, groups, organizations, and grantees and the desire to use their philanthropy to keep the family together. Both are valid goals but may be in dynamic tension. (And of course, there are ways of addressing both.) As one sets up a funding or foundation plan, it is crucial to be as self aware as possible which of these matters more.

- *Do you wish recognition OR do you prefer anonymity?*

There are those whose personal ethic or religious belief leads to a conviction that anonymity is a higher form of giving. But many other religious and ethics systems are built on a different concept of communal responsibility – that leadership requires modeling ones behavior so that others follow. In my work with individual philanthropists and philanthropic families, both approaches have been followed with credibility, impact, and satisfaction. What is important is to be honest with oneself about which and why.

- *What is your risk tolerance?*

Every philanthropic gift has an element of risk. In my teaching, I give examples of what appear to be risk free gifts that, much to everyone's surprise can bring embarrassment to the funder or yield a failed program. There is no such thing as "risk free." (Given the economy of the last year or so, no one needs convincing.) There are however relative levels of risk. Some argue that money for the public good deserves to be stewarded in the most prudent and cautious way. Support only the proven, quality institutions with demonstrable results.

Others have a different tolerance and approach: if philanthropic dollars are the vehicle for society to test out new ideas, then only private philanthropy can afford to experiment and justify failure. For example, innovation, by definition, is riskier than the well established. The results of innovative programs may be terrifically exciting and cutting edge, but have a greater likelihood of falling flat. If one has a high-risk tolerance, he or she is more likely to be an enthusiastic funder of innovation; if one doesn't, one would do well to stick to the proven.

- *Are you a "team player" or a "self starter"?*

In the days when I was the head of a foundation, the foundation was very committed to partnerships, collaborations, and joint efforts for a variety of very good reasons. One of my charges was to recruit other philanthropists and foundations to join us for some of these really fine and innovative programs. Some said yes and were wonderful partners, who were more than prepared to set aside their own autonomy for a greater good – at least for that project. Others were, frankly, not very good partners: they accepted the value of leveraging their resources to solve a problem but they were not very good team players. Their own priorities and procedures always took precedence over the collective.[21]

---

[21] Readers should feel free to contact me for a useful checklist to help you determine if you are likely to be a good collaborator or if a particular project lends itself to a partnership.

- *Do you want to be identified with a "prestigious" organization or be hands-on with a neighborhood one?*

Several years ago, after a lecture to a national wealth management conference, an attorney approached me about the problem one of his clients had. This client, whose name would be recognized by most readers of these essays, and whose net worth would allow gifts comparable to anyone, had been persuaded to join the board of one of the world's most prestigious institutions. After three years, this funder was only frustrated. When we met, the person told me "this has been such a waste of my time; I don't need to buy prestige but all they want is my check. If I am going to be involved in philanthropy, I want to be involved."

Now, you and I know well that, for many, to be on the board of such an organization would be the capstone of ones philanthropic career – a recognition that one can give, and has, at the highest levels, and that organizations which manifest the world's cultural heritage welcome you to its leadership.

But for this philanthropist, philanthropy was the opportunity to get his/her hands dirty – to be a key player in making a difference, not simply through largesse but more, by being there. Only you know which you are, but you will be awfully frustrated if you want to be at the decision making table, and all they really want is that you buy a table at the benefit.

- *Are you an "entrepreneur" or a "venture" funder?*

Let's be honest. Most funders have money to give because they have been successful. You have made money or been lucky enough to inherit it. But how you made that money can tell you a lot about what kind of philanthropy is going to work for you. If you spent a lifetime building a business from a storefront to a nationally prominent enterprise, you knew something about the patience necessary to create something over time and to weather the ebbs and flows of the economy and institution building. You are likely to respect the long view, the need to develop infrastructure, the benefit of consensus buy-in to a business model, and the value that scale can bring. You are likely to have a greater patience for and understanding of the societal benefit of the great intermediary type organizations – United Way, American Cancer Society, Jewish Federations, Catholic Charities, to name but a very few. You appreciate that such organizations take the long view, support institutions that can leverage philanthropic dollars, and cultivate leadership and funders over the long-term. Such organizations are typically consensus driven, and long-term commitment counts.

But, for lots and lots of people, especially younger ones, that is not the most gratifying way to do philanthropy. Nor is the way in which they made their money. If you are among the many who made money as a venture capitalist or in the hedge fund field or in certain other financial fields, your perspective is much shorter. Your commitment can be 3-5 years; it can be milliseconds. You aren't looking for lifetime commitment, only short-term turn around. Success isn't measured in infrastructure but in returns. And you surely haven't the patience to send all decisions to committees that must then approve, balance, compromise, and consensus every idea.

- *Do you want to be a local, regional, national or international player?*

The chair of the foundation I used to head participated in a group that was widely known as the mega-group. Initially I had assumed, as did most others, that the definition of a mega-philanthropist is one whose giving puts him or her in the top ranks of philanthropic giving each year. What I learned is that this was not exactly correct. To be sure, everyone who was invited to participate in that group gave (or their foundation did) at a

level which would inspire envy among the purely affluent and cause salivation among non-profits.

It was later, when I began to advise philanthropists
and families, that I learned that there were lots of others
who gave at least as much as those in the mega group
and not always secretly. It led me to wonder why were
some so identified with that appellation and others not
mentioned. What seemed to distinguish them was two
consistencies: that the mega-philanthropists wanted their
giving to be indentified with national or international
issues and that they didn't want their primary philanthropic shadow to be local.

Why? It seems that some funders want to see their
legacy in addressing larger and resistant issues of society
or at least some segment of it. By using their name or
reputation to focus on these matters, it refocuses away
from specific institutions and more to the problems to be
solved. For some, giving nationally and internationally,
as a focus, allows them to be exempted from the admit-
tedly messier choice of favoring one or more local organization over another. And some simply see themselves
as citizens of the world – why not have their philanthropy express that?

But, equally persuasive is that some funders specifically know that they can make a manifest and meaningful difference within their own communities. To see their
names on buildings, or to take leadership in local organizations, or to inspire their neighbors and friends to join
them is far more immediately gratifying. Involvement
nationally is typically an episodic venture; involvement
locally is typically daily.

This question has another implication for families. It
is rare indeed for families to all live in the same community. While we have discussed this question elsewhere, it
is important to realize that geographic focus has real implications for who gets involved, and who will care. A
family may have made its money in a single location,
and the founder has been a major funder there, if none of
the family remains in that community, what should be

focus of their funding be? This is worth clarifying up front.

As with other choices listed here, it isn't that one is more effective, credible, or preferable to the other. But it is important to know which seems to better reflect your style as a way to decide which organizations to fund and, more importantly, in which organizations or partnerships to assume an active role.

- *Do you like to "micro-manage" your grants or "fund and run?"*

Most of us, no matter what our means, "fund and run." The annual gift to our university, or to our church or synagogue, or to *United Way* or any of the myriad other causes most of us find ourselves giving to are, in this category. Most of us don't assume that we can or should take a very active role in every single organization we give something to.[22]

However, for some, that is neither satisfying nor reflective of what we want our philanthropy to be. For some, philanthropy means not only our money but also our time and heart. We want to be deeply involved in what we give to and want our involvement to matter, or at least make a difference.

If your interest is to support organizations and be left alone, there are many questions that can be ignored or at least obviated. But if your interest is to be involved, it requires several other considerations:

> ➤ The proportional scope of your gift. A $1000 gift to your alma mater isn't likely to get a lot of attention; a $1000 gift to a start up arts group may make you an officer of the Board.

---

[22] Some refer to this as "check book philanthropy."

➢ The ability to administer or the time to attend to a hands on approach. Reading proposals, doing due diligence, making site visits, understanding appropriate evaluation methods requires commitment. I once met with a new foundation that told me that they wanted to give lots of small gifts on a competitive basis and that they didn't want to have any staff people so there wouldn't be unnecessary overhead. They didn't realize the inherent contradiction in the two.

➢ The proportionality of expectation: in these days of accountability and outcomes, there is a tendency for funders to want grantees or even potential grantees to provide more and more information and evidence. And as a way to treat everyone equally, to ask all to do exactly the same. But in fact, a grant to a major research hospital is profoundly different from a grant to a small after school program. In the former, there are staff whose jobs it is to answer such questions; in the latter, there may be a few staff doing everything. Asking a teen worker to fill out monthly report forms may not only be inefficient, but it may well interfere with that person delivering the service for which he or she is trained. I believe it is important for those who want to manage their giving in a hands-on way to distinguish between equality and equitability.

➢ The culture of the organization being funded: like it or not, not every non-profit wants hands on donors. Whether that is right or wrong, a funder who really wants to be hands on should do some careful investigation whether he or she will be constantly at loggerheads with the staff and board. There are places that would cherish your involvement, so move on. And, most of all, be aware that it matters - to you.

➢ Perpetuity or sunset?

Step 2:
Formulating Your Mission

A n oft-repeated aphorism is, "If you don't know where you are going, any path will take you there." Certainly that is the funding strategy of most folks. After all, take a look at your list of charitable gifts last year? You may find a pattern – but you may not find a strategy. This next process will help take those patterns and give them a structure.

This process is well known to most foundations that accept proposals. It is the process of narrowing down the field and letting others, and yourselves, know what you truly do want to consider funding. For many, you have already done this, or some variation. Going through this process, as a second step, should prove very enlightening, especially since we put on the table a few categories that are often implicit but not articulated.

1. Geographic

We have already raised the issue of geography from a "culture" perspective. In this case, we invite you to think more proactively if location is a key component to setting priorities for your funding. It may be where you live, a place that reflects your heritage, a place where your family has roots, a place where your business is headquartered – or it may not matter at all.

If what you really care about is the cultural health of the community where you live, there is little reason to consider funding museums in a community 1000 miles away. It helps you, and your potential grantees if you are clear if geography matters.

2. Field of interest

Many funders are less interested in place or even specific organizations, but they care deeply about an issue, a challenge, a societal problem, a cultural interest. If that is your case, what will matter less are which organizations you fund than a specific project. If you are interested in after school literacy programs, you are going to find them of only marginally relevance if a community center has a proven record in senior adult service. If you were interested in research regarding housing for the homeless, you would probably not find a research hospital to be an enticing grantee.

I sit on the board of an entity that incubates innovation. Within broad outlines, the topic of the eligible groups is not the prime variable when being considered for participation, but their approach, how long the group has existed, and scope of what they hope to accomplish matters a lot.

3. Family or trustee interest(s)

Not infrequently, I have worked with families whose grantmaking pattern seems to belie any coherent pattern until I met with the family trustees. Sure enough, the pattern emerged quickly. What was being funded was simply an amalgam of the interests of those in the room.

Now, there are a number of functional questions to be asked about this kind of focus: why do it collectively at all if all that is being funded are personal projects? What are expectations regarding these priorities on subsequent trustees or generations? Does it matter if some of these grants are not accomplishing anything? When might a grant, given for personal interest reasons, be perceived to be veering into the conflict of interest realm?

But for some, giving this way and properly understood can serve a larger purpose: encourage communal leadership, enhance multi-generation family involvement, allow agility in responding to new or changing needs... Objectively, this may or may not be the most effective philanthropy, but if in fact a funder or foundation has a focus based primarily on the interests of the trustees, it is better for the trustees to be honest and open with each other than to pretend that there is objective basis for these strategies.

4. Institutional commitment

The opposite of #2. No surprise here: some funders really care about specific institutions. They believe in them or have benefited from them or admire them or have been a leader in them. The purpose of their funding vehicle or of their annual funding is clear and unequivocal. Such an approach may not be very empowering to other trustees, or encouraging to organizations not on the list, but it should lead to a very efficient funding process.

5. Long or short term

There are funders who will continue to fund the same organizations indefinitely. Others don't feel that grantees should ever expect funding for any project for more than, say, three years.[23]

When this is a primary focus of one's funding approach, it is a view of the underlying role of philanthropy or charitable giving. Typically, but not always, long-term commitments are likely to align with #4. Long-term funders are more inclined to believe in or be committed to particular institutions and organizations. They are more likely to be prepared to provide core funding to institutions, sit on the boards of those organizations, and require less support information in order to make a gift.

---

[23] I once knew of a funding collaborative that had a policy that they would never fund any organization for more than one year; fortunately, they eventually adjusted that upward.

Shorter-term funders are more likely to be committed to projects or innovation. They are more likely to use competitive processes for making decisions, look for greater amounts of information before making a decision, be structured in such a way (staff or very active trustees) that they can devote themselves to doing such due diligence, and view their giving as supplementary or experimental to the core budget of an organization.

6. Value based

"Social change," "democratic values," "eliminating poverty," "education for all," are examples of value-based focus for funding. It is the articulation and manifestation of a particular set of values that informs the decision-making. Such funders might fund long or short-term, provide core or project funding, give locally or internationally; those are details. (Not unimportant but not primary.) What is essential is that these funders have an articulated understanding of society and their role in getting to that vision.

7. You scratch my back...

I once was present when two fabulously wealthy bold face names solicited each other. The first asked for a specific amount for a project he cared about. The response was quite explicit: I will give you a check for that if you give me a check, for the same amount, for my project.[24]

If one is honest about helping funders address their underlying focus, one must add, "You scratch my back..." to the list. In many cases, funders see themselves as part of a peer social network. For the best of these, it is the belief in the impact that this group can have on a community, an organization, a societal prob-

---

[24] This was the most direct and overt quid pro quo solicitation I had ever seen.

lem that really makes a difference. Not everyone has the same priorities, but as a funder you know that there will come a time when your friend, colleague, or neighbor will come knocking. You give to their cause because they know that you will soon come knocking at their door and expect the same.

There are times, in fact, when the "you scratch my back" approach can lead to more innovative philanthropy. We wrote earlier about partnerships and collaborations as ways of leveraging dollars and influence. Invariably, such approaches will have a "lead" partner – the one who is most committed or who thought of the idea. It is possible that none would be willing to fund an experimental arts program, or a cutting edge after school program alone, but together they might.

Giving circles, a phenomenon about which much has been written and is now the basis for many contemporary youth philanthropy initiatives, is often based on mutuality of support. Several, but not all, projects get more funding than they might by a single funder – often funded because of a willingness to trust or yield to the passions of another member of the group.

Some will argue whether this is truly thoughtful or strategic giving. Or is it simply a set of social chits? Perhaps. But as with all other categories, it is important for a funder to be both self aware and honest with him or herself. If, at the end of the thought process, one decides that this is what will be the defining focus of ones giving, better to know it and build around it, than to have it be an unspoken elephant in the room.

Step 3:

Understanding Your Funding Culture

By this time, you already have a pretty strong sense of what makes your culture and your focus distinctive. Those who have ever done Meyers Briggs can begin to see how the different parts fit together. You can see why you instinctively lean positively toward some kinds of giving, and are left cold by other requests that, on the surface, seem equally justifiable. You can see why your fellow trustee at the table has very different responses to the very same proposal. And you can begin to extrapolate how to make your giving gratifying, and strategically appropriate to you, your family, or your foundation.

Now is the time to return to formulating your driving mission. At this point, a mission or vision statement should be able to convey your distinctiveness. It will not simply be a series of value words but a statement that conveys how and why you fund as you do.

Often, a mission is best understood as a legacy statement. In my own work, several families or small foundations decided that a classic mission statement would never be adequate to inform future decision makers. Rather they chose to append a history – of the family or the company that was the source of their wealth. What experiences, what values, what decisions, what influences brought them to this point. Hopefully great-grandchildren or future trustees, looking for direction in the face of competing claims, will be able to look back on this history, this legacy statement, as a way to make decisions.

Others found that, having gone through this process, creating a mission statement becomes very easy. It is now evident why a city or a field of interest or a kind of institution will always be favored. Just say so simply in a couple of sentences. When you have your own clarity of why you want to fund in certain ways, it is much easier to be clear to others.

And having done that, it is time to get down to the giving part... but that is for another time.

Afterword

- August 2009 -

Many of the pre-publication readers of this collection told me they felt that they were participating in an extended conversation. They could almost hear the give and take in many of the essays, and felt that the discussion was only just beginning.

No comments could have made me happier. Conversations are dynamic, and often unfinished. So I invite you to continue by reading my blog at *WisePhilanthropy.blogspot.com* or to be in touch directly, with your reactions to the many topics covered here – and to the many topics not yet covered.

Philanthropy, we know, is in the midst of very real profound challenges and changes. In such times, it sometimes becomes too easy to yield to polemics and fads. My hope is that we avoid those responses and continue to engage this uncharted territory together, developing best practices, innovative approaches, and responsible understandings of the role of private philanthropy throughout the world I look forward to doing so – in seminars, on the blog, in person – all in pursuit of making our world a more prefect place with the resources and wisdom within our grasp.

Until then…